NUTRIBULLET

RECIPE BOOK

The Ultimate Recipe Guide to Health and Wellness
Boost Your Energy and Immunity

Jessie Gardner

TABLE OF CONTENT

The "NutriBullet Recipe Cookbook" is a ground-breaking compilation that promises to alter the way you approach nutrition and wellbeing, and it features the ultimate culinary adventure for health enthusiasts and food lovers alike. This cookbook brings together two seemingly incompatible concepts—vibrant health and delicious food—and invites you on a culinary journey that successfully blends the two. This book is more than simply a collection of recipes; it's a road map to a better, longer life.

In a time when convenience is frequently prioritized over nutrition, the NutriBullet Recipe Cookbook is a welcome reminder that a tasty and healthy meal can be made with just one appliance. The tour kicks off with a deep dive into the revolutionary health and nutrition tool that is the NutriBullet. Whether you're a seasoned user of the NutriBullet or just starting out, our cookbook will be your go-to resource for making the most of this versatile kitchen appliance.

As you flip through the pages of this cookbook, you'll discover an abundance of dishes for every diet and eating style. We have everything you could possibly want to satisfy your hunger, from vibrant summer smoothie bowls to comforting winter soups. Our recipes include a broad range of tastes and cuisines, so you'll never get bored with your NutriBullet.

We know that people who are concerned with their health come from all walks of life, and our recipes reflect that. You'll find a wide variety of selections that cater to your specific dietary preferences, whether you're a strict vegetarian, an avid carnivore, or fall somewhere in between. Our recipes, which place an emphasis on fresh, whole foods, are designed to do more than just satisfy your taste buds; they will also provide your body with the nourishment it needs.

The NutriBullet's ability to keep foods' nutritious value intact is one of its most impressive qualities. You're not simply producing a smoothie when you use a NutriBullet; you're making a nutrient-rich work of art. We've made use of this potential by developing dishes that are not only tasty but also rich in healthy nutrients, including vitamins, minerals, and antioxidants. From immunity-boosting elixirs to metabolism-boosting potions, this cookbook has a wide variety of recipes to help you reach your health and fitness goals.

Time is of the essence in the modern society. That's why we've made it a point to provide recipes that aren't only healthy but also very practical. If you're a working professional, a mom with a full plate, or just someone who values their time, you'll love how quickly and easily you can whip up one of our meals. With the help of a NutriBullet, you can quickly and easily prepare healthy meals and snacks without compromising on taste or quality.

The NutriBullet Recipe Cookbook is more than just a collection of recipes; it's also a thorough introduction to the art and science of healthy eating. Several substances' positive effects on health and energy are explored in detail. You'll learn the secrets of macronutrient balance, the healing potential of superfoods, and the enchantment of herbs and spices. To help you adjust recipes to your personal tastes in terms of flavor and health, we've included some handy hints.

This cookbook's dedication to all-around health is its defining feature. We think you should practice healthy habits in all parts of your life, not just the kitchen. You will learn the transformational potential of nutrition for your body, mind, and soul as you begin your adventure with NutriBullet. We go into the idea of mindful eating, assisting you in developing a more meaningful relationship with the food you consume and the act of sustaining yourself.

The NutriBullet Recipe Cookbook is more than simply a cookbook; it's a comprehensive guide to a healthier, happier way of life. Whether you're looking to trim down, bulk up, or just enjoy the pleasure of making and eating nutritious cuisine, our cookbook will be your trusted companion on this gratifying path.

In conclusion, the NutriBullet Recipe Cookbook is proof that nutritious food can also be delicious and convenient. This cookbook is more than simply a useful resource for the kitchen; it is also a reliable friend in your search for better health and greater happiness, thanks to its wealth of delicious recipes, insightful nutritional information, and helpful hints. Join the NutriBullet movement and let the tasty flavors and healthy nutrients on these pages change your life. Welcoming you to a brand new era of culinary pleasure and health, the NutriBullet Recipe Cookbook.

CHAPTER:2 NUTRIBULLET BASICS AND TIPS

Start with the Right Ingredients:

Fresh fruits: Use a variety of fresh fruits like bananas, berries, mangoes, and apples.

Vegetables: Incorporate leafy greens (e.g., spinach kale) and other vegetables (e.g., carrots, cucumber) for added nutrients.

Liquid base: Use water, coconut water, almond milk, or yogurt as a liquid base for your smoothie.

Greek yogurt, tofu, or protein powder are all great sources of protein that may be added to your smoothie to up the satiety factor.

Add healthy fats and a velvety texture by blending in some avocado, flaxseeds, or nut butter.

To make your smoothie more filling and nutritious, try to strike a balance between carbs, proteins, and healthy fats in the ingredients.

Experiment with Flavors:

Add flavor and sweetness with ingredients like honey, agave nectar, vanilla extract, or cinnamon.

Don't be afraid to get creative with spices and herbs like ginger, mint, or basil.

Don't Overfill:

Don't fill your Nutribullet cup beyond the max fill line to avoid spills and overloading the motor.

Layer Ingredients:

Layer your ingredients in the cup for better blending. Start with liquids, followed by softer ingredients, and then harder ingredients on top.

Use Frozen Ingredients:

Frozen fruits and vegetables can make your smoothies colder and thicker without the need for ice.

Add Ice for Extra Chill:

If you want a super cold smoothie, add a handful of ice cubes.

Blend in Stages:

To ensure all ingredients are thoroughly blended, pulse, or blend in short bursts shake the cup between blends.

Customize to Your Needs:

Customize your Nutribullet recipes to suit your dietary preferences and nutritional needs. For example, add superfoods like chia seeds, spirulina, or acai for an extra nutrient boost.

Clean Your Nutribullet Promptly:

Rinse the blender cup and blades immediately after use to prevent ingredients from drying and sticking to the blades.

Safety First:

Always make sure the Nutribullet is properly assembled before blending, and follow the manufacturer's safety guidelines.

Start Simple:

If you're new to Nutribullet, start with basic recipes and gradually experiment with more complex combinations as you become more comfortable with the process.

Consider Texture:

Adjust the amount of liquid you use to achieve your desired smoothie thickness. More liquid will result in a thinner smoothie, while less liquid will make it thicker.

Portion Control:

Pay attention to portion sizes, as smoothies can be calorie-dense. Use smaller cups if you're watching your calorie intake.

Keep it Clean:

Regularly clean the blades, cups, and other parts of your Nutribullet to maintain hygiene and ensure optimal blending performance.

BERRY BANANA BLISS

Preparation Time: 5 minutes

Cooking Time: N/A

Serving: 2 servings

Ingredients:

- 1 ripe banana
- 1 cup mixed berries (strawberries, blueberries, raspberries)
- 1/2 cup low-fat yogurt (or dairy-free alternative for a vegan option)
- 1/2 cup almond milk (or any preferred milk)
- 1 tablespoon honey or maple syrup (adjust to taste)
- 1/2 cup ice cubes
- Fresh mint leaves for garnish (optional)

Instructions:

1. Put the ingredients together: If using fresh berries, properly wash the mixed berries and peel the ripe banana. Measure out the ice cubes, yogurt, almond milk, honey, or maple syrup.
2. It's Blended: Put the frozen berries, banana, low-fat yogurt, almond milk, honey (or maple syrup), and ice cubes into your Nutribullet blender.
3. Put everything together until it's smooth. When the batter is smooth and creamy, lock the lid of the blender and keep blending. If the batter is too thick, add a little more almond milk until it has the right consistency.
4. Serve: Two glasses should be filled with the Berry Banana Bliss smoothie. Adding fresh mint leaves as a garnish is optional.

GREEN GODDESS SMOOTHIE

Preparation Time: 7 minutes

Cooking Time: N/A

Serving: 2

Ingredients:

- 2 cups spinach leaves
- 1 ripe avocado, pitted and peeled
- 1/2 cucumber, peeled and chopped
- 1/2 lemon, juiced
- 1 cup coconut water
- 1 tablespoon chia seeds
- 1 cup ice cubes (optional)

Instructions:

1. Thoroughly wash the spinach leaves.
2. In your Nutribullet blender, combine the spinach, ripe avocado, finely sliced cucumber, lemon juice, coconut water, chia seeds, and ice cubes (if using).
3. The mixture should be smooth and creamy after about 45 seconds of blending at high speed.
4. Pour glasses with the Green Goddess Smoothie inside.
5. If you'd like, add a slice of lemon or cucumber as a garnish.
6. Serve right away to enjoy the freshness!

TROPICAL SUNRISE DELIGHT

Preparation Time: 6 minutes

Cooking Time: N/A

Serving: 2

Ingredients:

- 1 cup pineapple chunks
- 1/2 cup mango chunks
- 1 ripe banana
- 1/2 cup coconut milk
- 1/2 cup orange juice
- 1 tablespoon honey
- 1/2 cup ice cubes (optional)

Instructions:

1. To your Nutribullet blender, add the pineapple pieces, mango chunks, ripe banana, coconut milk, orange juice, honey, and ice cubes (if using).
2. About 40 seconds, or when the mixture is smooth and tropical, blend at high speed.
3. Pour glasses with the Tropical Sunrise Delight.
4. For a bright touch, garnish with a piece of pineapple or an orange wedge.
5. Serve right now and escape to a paradise in the tropics!

PEANUT BUTTER POWER PUNCH

Preparation Time: 5 minutes

Cooking Time: N/A

Serving: 1

Ingredients:

- 1 ripe banana
- 2 tablespoons of natural peanut butter
- 1/2 cup of low-fat Greek yogurt
- 1/2 cup of unsweetened almond milk
- 1 tablespoon of honey
- 1 tablespoon of flaxseeds
- 1/2 cup of ice cubes

Instructions:

1. Place the peeled banana in the Nutribullet cup.
2. Honey, flaxseeds, unsweetened almond milk, natural peanut butter, low-fat Greek yogurt, and ice cubes should all be added.
3. Blend till creamy and smooth.
4. Pour your Peanut Butter Power Punch into a glass, then sip.

OATMEAL COOKIE CRUNCH

Preparation Time: 5 minutes

Cooking Time: N/A

Serving: 1

Ingredients:

- 1/2 cup of rolled oats
- 1/2 cup of unsweetened vanilla almond milk
- 1 ripe banana
- 1/2 teaspoon of ground cinnamon
- 1/4 teaspoon of vanilla extract
- 1 tablespoon of honey
- 1/4 cup of crushed walnuts
- 1/4 cup of raisins
- 1/2 cup of ice cubes

Instructions:

1. The Nutribullet cup should be filled with rolled oats.
2. A ripe banana, ground cinnamon, vanilla essence, honey, chopped walnuts, raisins, and ice cubes should all be included.
3. Blend until well combined and creamy.
4. Enjoy the Oatmeal Cookie Crunch after pouring it into a glass!

SPINACH AND STRAWBERRY SWIRL

Preparation Time: 5 minutes

Cooking Time: N/A

Serving: 1

Ingredients:

- 1 cup of fresh spinach leaves
- 1/2 cup of fresh strawberries
- 1/2 cup of low-fat vanilla yogurt
- 1/2 cup of unsweetened apple juice
- 1 tablespoon of honey
- 1/2 cup of ice cubes

Instructions:

1. Put the Nutribullet cup with the fresh spinach leaves inside.
2. Include honey, ice cubes, low-fat vanilla yogurt, unsweetened apple juice, fresh strawberries, and low-fat yogurt.
3. Blend the ingredients until it's vivid and smooth.
4. Pour the spinach and strawberry swirl into a glass, and enjoy!

BLUEBERRY BLAST OFF

Preparation Time: 5 minutes

Cook Time: 0 minutes (This is a no-cook smoothie)

Serving: 1

Ingredients:

- 1 cup fresh or frozen blueberries
- 1/2 banana, peeled
- 1/2 cup Greek yogurt
- 1/2 cup almond milk
- 1 tablespoon honey (optional)
- 1/2 teaspoon vanilla extract
- 1 cup ice cubes

Instructions:

1. In the Nutribullet blender, combine the blueberries, banana, Greek yogurt, almond milk, honey (if using), and vanilla extract.
2. Over the other ingredients, add the ice cubes.
3. Secure the cover on the blender and run it on high for 45 to 60 seconds or until the mixture is smooth and the bright blueberry color is visible.
4. Enjoy this smoothie packed with antioxidants by pouring the Blueberry Blast Off into a glass and garnishing it with a few fresh blueberries.

MANGO TANGO TWIST

Preparation Time: 5 minutes

Cook Time: 0 minutes (This is a no-cook smoothie)

Serving: 1

Ingredients:

- 1 cup ripe mango chunks (fresh or frozen)
- 1/2 cup pineapple chunks
- 1/2 cup Greek yogurt
- 1/4 cup orange juice
- 1 tablespoon honey (optional)
- 1/2 teaspoon lime juice
- 1 cup ice cubes

Instructions:

1. The Nutribullet blender should be filled with mango and pineapple chunks, Greek yogurt, orange juice, honey (if wanted), and lime juice.
2. Over the other ingredients, add the ice cubes.
3. Fasten the blender's cover and blend the ingredients for 45-60 seconds or until smooth and the tropical flavors are evenly distributed.
4. Pour the Mango Tango Twist into a glass to enjoy this delicious smoothie while feeling exotic!

ALMOND JOY ELIXIR

Preparation Time: 5 minutes

Cook Time: 0 minutes (This is a no-cook smoothie)

Serving: 1

Ingredients:

- 1/2 cup unsweetened coconut milk
- 1/2 cup almond milk
- 2 tablespoons cocoa powder
- 2 tablespoons almond butter
- 1 tablespoon honey (optional)
- 1/4 teaspoon coconut extract
- 1/2 cup ice cubes

Instructions:

1. In the Nutribullet blender, combine the coconut milk, almond milk, cocoa powder, almond butter, honey (if preferred), and coconut extract.
2. Over the other ingredients, add the ice cubes.
3. Fasten the blender's cover and blend the ingredients on high for 45 to 60 seconds or until silky smooth and tasting as luscious as an Almond Joy.
4. Pour the Almond Joy Elixir into a glass, then indulge in this delicious pleasure guilt-free!

PEACHY KEEN REFRESHER

Preparation Time: 5 minutes

Cook Time: None

Serving: 1

Ingredients:

- 1 ripe peach, pitted and sliced
- 1/2 cup Greek yogurt
- 1/2 cup unsweetened almond milk
- 1 tablespoon honey
- 1/4 teaspoon vanilla extract
- 1/2 cup ice cubes
- A squeeze of fresh lemon juice (optional)

Instructions:

1. In your Nutribullet blender, combine the sliced peach, Greek yogurt, almond milk, honey, vanilla essence, and ice cubes.
2. If more zing is wanted, squeeze in more fresh lemon juice.
3. Blend the ingredients for generally 30 to 45 seconds or until it is smooth and creamy. Secure the blender top.
4. Pour the Peachy Keen Refresher into a glass, top with a slice of peach, and savor this energizing treat!

RASPBERRY ZEST FUSION

Preparation Time: 5 minutes

Cook Time: None

Serving: 1

Ingredients:

- 1/2 cup fresh raspberries
- 1/2 cup chopped pineapple
- 1/2 cup spinach leaves
- 1/2 cup coconut water
- 1 tablespoon chia seeds
- 1/2 cup ice cubes

Instructions:

1. In your Nutribullet blender, combine the raspberries, diced pineapple, spinach leaves, coconut water, chia seeds, and ice cubes.
2. Secure the lid on the blender, then blend for 45 to 60 seconds or until the mixture is smooth and the brilliant colors are combined.
3. Pour the Raspberry Zest Fusion into a glass, top with a few optional chia seeds for texture, and savor this flavorful and healthy fusion!

KIWI KICKSTART SMOOTHIE

Preparation Time: 5 minutes

Cook Time: None

Serving: 1

Ingredients:

- 2 ripe kiwis, peeled and sliced
- 1/2 banana
- 1/2 cup spinach leaves
- 1/2 cup unsweetened coconut milk
- 1 tablespoon honey
- 1/2 cup ice cubes

Instructions:

1. In your Nutribullet blender, combine the sliced kiwis, banana, spinach leaves, coconut milk, honey, and ice cubes.
2. Secure the lid on the blender, then blend for 45 to 60 seconds or until the mixture is smooth and a bright green color appears.
3. Enjoy this invigorating and delicious way to start your day by pouring the Kiwi Kickstart Smoothie into a glass and garnishing it with a piece of kiwi.

PINEAPPLE PARADISE POTION

Preparation Time: 5 minutes

Cook Time: N/A

Serving: 1

Ingredients:

- 1 cup fresh pineapple chunks
- 1/2 cup coconut milk
- 1/2 cup Greek yogurt
- 1 tablespoon honey
- 1/4 teaspoon grated ginger (optional)
- 1/2 cup ice cubes

Instructions:

1. The Nutribullet blender should be filled with fresh pineapple chunks, coconut milk, Greek yogurt, honey, and chopped ginger (if using).
2. Over the other ingredients, add the ice cubes.
3. Secure the cover on the blender, then blend the mixture on high for 45 to 60 seconds or until it is smooth and smells like a tropical paradise.
4. With this delicious smoothie, add the Pineapple Paradise Potion to a glass and escape to a warm beach!

CINNAMON ROLL DELIGHT

Preparation Time: 5 minutes

Cook Time: N/A

Serving: 1

Ingredients:

- 1/2 cup rolled oats
- 1 cup unsweetened almond milk
- 1/2 banana, peeled
- 1/2 teaspoon ground cinnamon
- 1/4 teaspoon vanilla extract
- 1 tablespoon maple syrup
- 1 tablespoon almond butter
- 1 cup ice cubes

Instructions:

1. In the Nutribullet blender, combine the rolled oats, almond milk, banana, ground cinnamon, vanilla extract, maple syrup, and almond butter.
2. Over the other ingredients, add the ice cubes.
3. For typically between 45 and 60 seconds, lock the blender top and blend the ingredients on high until it is smooth and tastes comfortingly like a cinnamon bun.
4. Pour the Cinnamon Roll Delight into a glass, top with a touch of cinnamon, and enjoy this delectable treat guilt-free!

COCONUT CREAM DREAM

Preparation Time: 5 minutes

Cook Time: N/A

Serving: 1

Ingredients:

- 1/2 cup coconut milk
- 1/2 cup pineapple chunks
- 1/2 banana, peeled
- 2 tablespoons shredded coconut
- 1 tablespoon honey
- 1/4 teaspoon vanilla extract
- 1/2 cup ice cubes

Instructions:

1. Put the banana, shredded coconut, coconut milk, pineapple chunks, honey, and vanilla essence in the Nutribullet blender.
2. The ice cubes should be added on top of the other components.
3. The mixture should be smooth and have a tropical coconut dreaminess after about 45 to 60 seconds of high-speed blending with the lid securely fastened.
4. Pour the Coconut Cream Dream into a glass, if preferred, decorate with more shredded coconut, and enjoy the creamy coconut flavor!

CHIA SEED ENERGY BOOST

Preparation Time: 5 minutes

Cook Time: N/A

Serving: 1

Ingredients:

- 1 cup unsweetened almond milk
- 2 tablespoons chia seeds
- 1/2 cup mixed berries (strawberries, blueberries, raspberries)
- 1/2 banana, peeled
- 1 tablespoon honey
- 1/4 teaspoon vanilla extract
- 1/2 cup ice cubes

Instructions:

1. In the Nutribullet blender, combine the almond milk, chia seeds, mixed berries, banana, honey, and vanilla extract.
2. Over the other ingredients, add the ice cubes.
3. Secure the cover on the blender, then blend the mixture on high for 45 to 60 seconds or until it is smooth and full of delicious energy-boosting ingredients.
4. Enjoy a healthy and stimulating start to your day by pouring the Chia Seed Energy Boost into a glass.

NUTTY CHOCOLATE DELIGHT

Preparation Time: 5 minutes

Cook Time: N/A

Serving: 1

Ingredients:

- 1 ripe banana
- 1 tablespoon unsweetened cocoa powder
- 2 tablespoons almond butter
- 1 cup unsweetened almond milk
- 1 tablespoon honey
- 1/2 teaspoon vanilla extract
- 1 cup ice cubes

Instructions:

1. In the Nutribullet blender, combine the banana, cocoa powder, almond butter, almond milk, honey, vanilla extract, and ice cubes.
2. Secure the cover on the blender, then blend the mixture on high for 30 to 45 seconds or until it is smooth and creamy.
3. Pour the Nutty Chocolate Delight into a glass, top with a slice of banana or a dusting of cocoa powder, and savor this decadent treat!

ORANGE CREAMSICLE SURPRISE

Preparation Time: 5 minutes

Cook Time: N/A

Serving: 1

Ingredients:

- 1 large orange, peeled and segmented
- 1/2 cup Greek yogurt

- 1 tablespoon honey
- 1/2 teaspoon vanilla extract
- 1/2 cup ice cubes

Instructions:

1. In the Nutribullet blender, combine the orange segments, Greek yogurt, honey, vanilla essence, and ice cubes.
2. Secure the cover of the blender, then blend the mixture on high for 30 to 45 seconds or until it is creamy and smooth.
3. Fill a glass with the Orange Creamsicle Surprise and savor the zesty, zingy tastes!

SPINACH AND PINEAPPLE PERFECTION

Preparation Time: 5 minutes

Cook Time: N/A

Serving: 1

Ingredients:

- 1 cup fresh spinach leaves
- 1/2 cup pineapple chunks (fresh or frozen)
- 1/2 banana, peeled
- 1/2 cup coconut water
- 1/2 cup water
- 1 cup ice cubes

Instructions:

1. Put the Nutribullet blender filled with fresh spinach leaves, pineapple chunks, banana, coconut water, water, and ice cubes.
2. Close the blender's cover and blend the ingredients for 45-60 seconds or until completely smooth and a vibrant green color.
3. Place some Spinach and Pineapple Perfection in a glass, and savor this deliciously healthy and tropical treat!

BANANA NUT BREAD BLISS

Preparation Time: 5 minutes

Cook Time: N/A

Serving: 1

Ingredients:

- 1 ripe banana
- 2 tablespoons chopped walnuts
- 1/2 teaspoon ground cinnamon
- 1/4 teaspoon nutmeg
- 1 cup unsweetened almond milk
- 1/2 cup Greek yogurt
- 1 tablespoon honey
- 1 cup ice cubes

Instructions:

1. In the Nutribullet blender, combine the ripe banana, chopped walnuts, cinnamon, nutmeg, almond milk, Greek yogurt, honey, and ice cubes.
2. Affix the cover to the blender, then blend the ingredients on high for 45 to 60 seconds or until the mixture is smooth and flavorful, like banana nut bread.
3. The Banana Nut Bread Bliss should be poured into a glass, garnished with cinnamon or a slice of banana, and then enjoyed.

MOCHA MADNESS MARVEL

Preparation Time: 5 minutes

Cook Time: N/A

Serving: 1

Ingredients:

- 1 cup brewed coffee, cooled
- 1/2 cup unsweetened almond milk
- 1 tablespoon unsweetened cocoa powder
- 1 tablespoon almond butter
- 1 tablespoon honey
- 1/2 teaspoon vanilla extract
- 1 cup ice cubes

Instructions:

1. Pour a cup of coffee into a separate container to chill.
2. In the Nutribullet blender, combine the ice cubes, cooled coffee, almond milk, chocolate powder, almond butter, honey, and vanilla extract.
3. Secure the cover of the blender, then blend the mixture on high for 30 to 45 seconds or until it is smooth and flavorful of rich mocha.
4. Pour some Mocha Madness Marvel into a glass, then savor this delicious coffee treat!

POMEGRANATE PASSION POTION

Preparation Time: 5 minutes

Cook Time: N/A

Serving: 1

Ingredients:

- 1/2 cup pomegranate seeds (or 1/4 cup pomegranate juice)
- 1/2 cup plain Greek yogurt
- 1/4 cup orange juice
- 1/4 cup water
- 1 tablespoon honey
- 1/2 cup ice cubes

Instructions:

1. Extraction of pomegranate seeds is required for utilizing them.
2. In the Nutribullet blender, combine the pomegranate seeds (or pomegranate juice), Greek yogurt, orange juice, water, honey, and ice cubes.
3. Blend the mixture on high for 45 to 60 seconds, or until it is smooth and a brilliant green color, with the lid securely on the blender.
4. Fill a glass with the Pomegranate Passion Potion, and savor this tart and revitalizing combination!

APPLE PIE IN A GLASS

Preparation Time: 5 minutes

Cook Time: N/A

Serving: 1

Ingredients:

- 1 apple, cored and sliced
- 1/2 cup rolled oats
- 1/2 teaspoon ground cinnamon
- 1/4 teaspoon nutmeg
- 1 tablespoon honey
- 1 cup unsweetened almond milk
- 1/2 cup ice cubes

Instructions:

1. In the Nutribullet blender, combine the apple slices, rolled oats, cinnamon, nutmeg, honey, almond milk, and ice cubes.
2. Lock the lid of the blender and blend the mixture on high for 45 to 60 seconds or until it is smooth and tastes deliciously like apple pie.
3. Enjoy this nutritious and cozy smoothie by pouring the Apple Pie into a glass and topping it with some cinnamon or an apple slice.

AVOCADO AVENGER SMOOTHIE

Preparation Time: 5 minutes

Cook Time: N/A

Serving: 1

Ingredients:

- 1/2 ripe avocado
- 1/2 banana, peeled
- 1 cup spinach leaves
- 1/2 cup unsweetened almond milk
- 1 tablespoon honey
- 1/2 cup ice cubes

Instructions:

1. Half of a ripe avocado should have the flesh removed.
2. In the Nutribullet blender, combine the avocado, banana, spinach leaves, almond milk, honey, and ice cubes.
3. Secure the cover of the blender, then blend the mixture on high for 45 to 60 seconds or until it is creamy and smooth.
4. Enjoy this creamy and nourishing green smoothie by pouring the Avocado Avenger Smoothie into a glass.

CARROT CAKE CONCOCTION

Preparation Time: 5 minutes

Cook Time: N/A

Serving: 1

Ingredients:

- 1 large carrot, peeled and chopped
- 1/2 cup plain Greek yogurt
- 1/4 cup rolled oats
- 1 tablespoon honey
- 1/2 teaspoon ground cinnamon
- 1/4 teaspoon nutmeg
- 1/2 cup almond milk
- 1/2 cup ice cubes

Instructions:

1. The Nutribullet blender should be filled with Greek yogurt, rolled oats, honey, cinnamon, nutmeg, and almond milk.
2. Secure the cover on the blender, then blend the mixture on high for 45 to 60 seconds or until it is smooth and tastes deliciously like carrot cake.
3. Enjoy this smoothie that was inspired by dessert by pouring the Carrot Cake Concoction into a glass and adding some cinnamon or a piece of carrot as a garnish.

CHERRY ALMOND SWIRL

Preparation Time: 5 minutes

Cook Time: N/A

Serving: 1

Ingredients:

- 1/2 cup frozen cherries
- 2 tablespoons almond butter
- 1/2 cup plain Greek yogurt
- 1 tablespoon honey
- 1/2 teaspoon vanilla extract
- 1/2 cup unsweetened almond milk
- 1/2 cup ice cubes

Instructions:

1. In the Nutribullet blender, combine the frozen cherries, almond butter, Greek yogurt, honey, vanilla extract, almond milk, and ice cubes.
2. When the liquid is smooth and has a delicious cherry-almond swirl, often after around 30-45 seconds of blending on high, lock the cover of the blender.
3. Fill a glass with the Cherry Almond Swirl and savor the sweet and nutty flavor combination!

LEMON GINGER ENERGIZER

Preparation Time: 5 minutes

Cook Time: N/A

Serving: 1

Ingredients:

- 1 cup water
- 1/2 lemon, peeled and seeds removed
- 1-inch piece of fresh ginger, peeled
- 1 tablespoon honey (adjust to taste)
- 1 cup ice cubes

Instructions:

1. Lemon, ginger, honey, and water should all be added to the Nutribullet.
2. Ice cubes are added.
3. Blend on high, with the top securely fastened, for 30 to 45 seconds or until the mixture is smooth and frothy.
4. Enjoy the delicious and energizing energy boost by pouring the Lemon Ginger Energizer into a glass.

BEETROOT BEAUTY BOOSTER

Preparation Time: 7 minutes

Cook Time: N/A

Serving: 1

Ingredients:

- 1 small beetroot, peeled and chopped
- 1/2 cup Greek yogurt
- 1/2 cup mixed berries (strawberries, blueberries, raspberries)
- 1 tablespoon honey
- 1/2 teaspoon vanilla extract
- 1/2 cup water
- 1 cup ice cubes

Instructions:

1. The Nutribullet blender should be filled with diced beets, Greek yogurt, mixed berries, honey, vanilla extract, and water.
2. On top, place the ice cubes.
3. Lock the lid of the blender and blend the mixture on high for 60 to 90 seconds or until it is smooth and vivid.
4. Enjoy the benefits of this healthy smoothie's beauty-enhancing properties by pouring the Beetroot Beauty Booster into a glass.

BLACKBERRY BASIL BLISS

Preparation Time: 5 minutes

Cook Time: N/A

Serving: 1

Ingredients:

- 1 cup blackberries
- 4-5 fresh basil leaves
- 1/2 cup unsweetened almond milk
- 1/2 cup Greek yogurt
- 1 tablespoon honey
- 1/2 cup ice cubes

Instructions:

1. In the Nutribullet blender, combine blackberries, fresh basil leaves, almond milk, Greek yogurt, and honey.
2. Ice cubes are added.
3. For about 45–60 seconds, or until the mixture is smooth and the basil and blackberries are thoroughly combined, lock the cover of the blender in place.
4. Fill a glass with the Blackberry Basil Bliss and savor the unusual and revitalizing mix!

PUMPKIN PIE PLEASURE

Preparation Time: 8 minutes

Cook Time: N/A

Serving: 1

Ingredients:

- 1/2 cup canned pumpkin puree
- 1/2 banana, peeled
- 1/2 cup unsweetened almond milk
- 1 tablespoon maple syrup
- 1/2 teaspoon pumpkin pie spice
- 1/2 teaspoon vanilla extract
- 1 cup ice cubes

Instructions:

1. In the Nutribullet blender, combine the pumpkin puree, banana, almond milk, maple syrup, pumpkin pie spice, and vanilla extract.
2. Ice cubes are added.
3. When the mixture is smooth and tastes like pumpkin pie, secure the cover of the blender and process on high for typically 45 to 60 seconds.
4. Pour some Pumpkin Pie Pleasure into a glass of nutritious smoothie, and enjoy the taste of fall!

CRANBERRY ORANGE CRUSH

Preparation Time: 5 minutes

Cook Time: N/A

Serving: 1

Ingredients:

- 1/2 cup fresh or frozen cranberries
- 1 orange, peeled and seeds removed
- 1/2 cup Greek yogurt
- 1 tablespoon honey
- 1/2 cup water
- 1 cup ice cubes

Instructions:

1. In the Nutribullet blender, combine the cranberries, orange that has been peeled, Greek yogurt, honey, and water.
2. Ice cubes are added.
3. For approximately 45 to 60 seconds, or until the mixture is smooth and the cranberries are smashed, lock the cover of the blender in place and process on high.
4. Fill a glass with the Cranberry Orange Crush and savor the tart and energizing deliciousness!

HAZELNUT HEAVEN SMOOTHIE

Preparation Time: 5 minutes

Cook Time: N/A

Serving: 1

Ingredients:

- 1/4 cup hazelnuts
- 1 banana, peeled
- 1 tablespoon cocoa powder
- 1 tablespoon honey
- 1/2 cup unsweetened almond milk
- 1/2 cup ice cubes

Instructions:

1. In the Nutribullet blender, combine the hazelnuts, banana, chocolate powder, honey, almond milk, and ice cubes.
2. Securing the lid of the blender, blend the ingredients for 45 to 60 seconds on high or until it is smooth and creamy.
3. Fill a glass with the Hazelnut Heaven Smoothie and savor the luscious, nutty flavor!

WATERMELON WONDER BLAST

Preparation Time: 5 minutes

Cook Time: N/A

Serving: 1

Ingredients:

- 2 cups fresh watermelon chunks
- 1/2 lime, peeled and seeds removed
- 1/4 cup fresh mint leaves
- 1 tablespoon honey
- 1/2 cup ice cubes

Instructions:

1. In the Nutribullet blender, combine the watermelon pieces, lime, mint leaves, honey, and ice cubes.
2. For about 30-45 seconds, blend the mixture on high until it is smooth and the watermelon and mint are well combined.
3. Fill a glass with the Watermelon Wonder Blast and enjoy the cool flavor of summer!

PEACHES AND CREAM SUPREME

Preparation Time: 5 minutes

Cook Time: N/A

Serving: 1

Ingredients:

- 1 cup fresh or frozen peaches
- 1/2 cup Greek yogurt
- 1 tablespoon honey
- 1/2 teaspoon vanilla extract
- 1/2 cup unsweetened almond milk
- 1 cup ice cubes

Instructions:

1. In the Nutribullet blender, combine peaches, Greek yogurt, honey, vanilla extract, almond milk, and ice cubes.
2. Blend the ingredients on high for 45–60 seconds until fully smooth and creamy. Cover the blender.
3. Enjoy the delicious and velvety treat after pouring the Peaches and Cream Supreme into a glass!

STRAWBERRY SHORTCAKE SENSATION

Preparation Time: 5 minutes

Cook Time: N/A

Serving: 1

Ingredients:

- 1 cup fresh or frozen strawberries
- 1/2 cup Greek yogurt
- 1/4 cup rolled oats
- 1 tablespoon honey
- 1/2 teaspoon vanilla extract
- 1/2 cup unsweetened almond milk
- 1 cup ice cubes

Instructions:

1. In the Nutribullet blender, combine the strawberries, Greek yogurt, oats, honey, vanilla extract, almond milk, and ice cubes.
2. For 45 to 60 seconds on high, or until the mixture is smooth and resembles a strawberry shortcake, secure the cover of the blender.
3. Enjoy the dessert-like flavor of the Strawberry Shortcake Sensation in a glass of nutritious smoothie!

RASPBERRY LEMONADE REFRESHER

Preparation Time: 5 minutes

Cook Time: N/A

Serving: 1

Ingredients:

- 1/2 cup fresh or frozen raspberries
- 1 lemon, peeled and seeds removed
- 1/4 cup fresh mint leaves
- 1 tablespoon honey
- 1/2 cup water
- 1 cup ice cubes

Instructions:

1. In the Nutribullet blender, combine raspberries, a lemon that has been peeled, mint leaves, honey, water, and ice cubes.
2. Lock the lid of the blender and blend the mixture on high for 45 to 60 seconds, or until it is smooth and the raspberry and lemon tastes have combined.
3. Enjoy the tangy and energizing Raspberry Lemonade Refresher by pouring some into a glass.

SPINACH AND BLUEBERRY BURST

Preparation Time: 5 minutes

Cook Time: N/A

Serving: 1

Ingredients:

- 1 cup fresh spinach leaves
- 1/2 cup blueberries (fresh or frozen)
- 1/2 banana
- 1/2 cup Greek yogurt
- 1 tablespoon honey
- 1/2 cup water
- 1 cup ice cubes

Instructions:

1. Your Nutribullet blender should be filled with fresh spinach leaves, blueberries, bananas, Greek yogurt, honey, water, and ice cubes.
2. Lock the lid of the blender and blend the mixture on high for 45 to 60 seconds or until it is smooth and vivid.
3. Fill a glass with the Spinach and Blueberry Burst, and savor the reviving tastes and benefits!

BANANA SPLIT SIPPER

Preparation Time: 5 minutes

Cook Time: N/A

Serving: 1

Ingredients:

- 1 banana
- 1/2 cup strawberries (fresh or frozen)
- 1/4 cup pineapple chunks
- 1/2 cup unsweetened coconut milk
- 1 tablespoon chocolate syrup
- 1 tablespoon chopped nuts (walnuts or almonds)
- Whipped cream (optional)
- Maraschino cherry (optional)

Instructions:

1. In the Nutribullet blender, combine the banana, strawberries, pineapple pieces, coconut milk, and chocolate syrup.
2. To make a smooth and creamy smoothie, place all the ingredients in a blender and cover it. Blend on high for 45-60 seconds.
3. The Banana Split Sipper should be poured into a glass topped with whipped cream (if preferred), chopped almonds, and a maraschino cherry for the authentic banana split finish.

MANGO CHILI CHILLER

Preparation Time: 5 minutes

Cook Time: N/A

Serving: 1

Ingredients:

- 1 cup ripe mango chunks (fresh or frozen)
- 1/2 cup plain Greek yogurt
- 1/4 teaspoon chili powder
- 1 tablespoon honey
- 1/2 cup coconut water
- 1 cup ice cubes
- Lime wedge for garnish (optional)

Instructions:

1. In the Nutribullet blender, combine the mango chunks, Greek yogurt, chili powder, honey, coconut water, and ice cubes.
2. When the combination is smooth, and the chili has a sufficient amount of heat, secure the lid of the blender and process the mixture for 45 to 60 seconds on high.
3. Pour the Mango Chili Chiller into a glass, add a lime wedge as a garnish (if preferred), and savor the combination of sweetness and spiciness!

PEANUT BUTTER AND JELLY JOY

Preparation Time: 5 minutes

Cook Time: N/A

Serving: 1

Ingredients:

- 2 tablespoons natural peanut butter
- 1/2 cup mixed berries (strawberries, blueberries, raspberries)
- 1/2 banana
- 1 cup almond milk
- 1 tablespoon honey
- 1/2 teaspoon vanilla extract
- 1 cup ice cubes

Instructions:

1. In the Nutribullet blender, combine natural peanut butter, mixed berries, banana, almond milk, honey, vanilla extract, and ice cubes.
2. Lock the lid of the blender and blend the mixture on high for 45 to 60 seconds or until it is smooth and resembles a traditional PB&J sandwich.
3. In a glass, pour the Peanut Butter and Jelly Joy, and enjoy the flavor and reminiscence!

CLASSIC GREEN GODDESS SMOOTHIE

Preparation Time: 5 minutes

Cook Time: None

Serving: 1

Ingredients:

- 1 cup spinach leaves
- 1/2 cucumber, peeled and sliced
- 1/2 avocado, peeled and pitted
- 1/2 cup Greek yogurt
- 1/2 cup pineapple chunks
- 1/2 lemon, juiced
- 1 cup ice cubes

Instructions:

1. In your Nutribullet blender, combine spinach leaves, cucumber, avocado, Greek yogurt, pineapple pieces, lemon juice, and ice cubes.
2. To make a smooth and creamy smoothie, place all the ingredients in a blender and cover it. Blend on high for 45-60 seconds.
3. Pour some of the Classic Green Goddess Smoothie into a glass, and savor the flavor of tropical fruits and greens!

TROPICAL PARADISE GREENS

Preparation Time: 5 minutes

Cook Time: None

Serving: 1

Ingredients:

- 1 cup kale leaves
- 1/2 cup mango chunks
- 1/2 banana
- 1/2 cup coconut water

- 1 tablespoon chia seeds (optional)
- 1 cup ice cubes

Instructions:

1. In your Nutribullet blender, combine the kale leaves, mango chunks, banana, coconut water, chia seeds (if using), and ice cubes.
2. For about 45 to 60 seconds, or when the mixture is smooth and tropical-flavored, secure the cover of the blender and run it on high.
3. As you sip these Tropical Paradise Greens, picture yourself relaxing in a tropical paradise.

SPINACH PINEAPPLE DELIGHT

Preparation Time: 5 minutes

Cook Time: None

Serving: 1

Ingredients:

- 1 cup spinach leaves
- 1/2 cup pineapple chunks
- 1/2 banana
- 1/2 cup unsweetened almond milk
- 1 tablespoon honey (optional)
- 1 cup ice cubes

Instructions:

1. In your Nutribullet blender, combine the spinach leaves, pineapple pieces, banana, almond milk, honey (if using), and ice cubes.
2. Secure the cover of the blender, then blend the mixture on high for 45 to 60 seconds or until it is smooth and deliciously sweet and green.
3. Take a sip of the spinach pineapple delight while enjoying the exotic tastes.

KALE AND BANANA BLISS

Preparation Time: 5 minutes

Cook Time: None

Serving: 1

Ingredients:

- 1 cup kale leaves
- 1 banana
- 1/2 cup plain Greek yogurt
- 1/2 cup almond milk
- 1 tablespoon almond butter
- 1 tablespoon honey (optional)
- 1 cup ice cubes

Instructions:

1. In your Nutribullet blender, combine the kale leaves, banana, Greek yogurt, almond milk, almond butter, honey (if using), and ice cubes.
2. Fasten the blender's lid and blend the ingredients for 45-60 seconds or until silky smooth and creamy.
3. Experience the delightful fusion of kale and banana by pouring the Kale and Banana Bliss into a glass.

CUCUMBER MINT REFRESHER

Preparation Time: 5 minutes

Cook Time: None

Serving: 1

Ingredients:

- 1 cucumber, peeled and sliced
- 1/4 cup fresh mint leaves
- 1/2 lemon, juiced
- 1/2 cup water
- 1 tablespoon honey (optional)
- 1 cup ice cubes

Instructions:

1. In your Nutribullet blender, combine cucumber slices, fresh mint leaves, lemon juice, water, honey (if using), and ice cubes.
2. When the combination is smooth and very refreshing, often after approximately 45 to 60 seconds of blending on high, lock the blender cover.
3. Enjoy the invigorating flavor of cucumber and mint after pouring the cucumber mint refresher into a glass.

AVOCADO SPINACH DREAM

Preparation Time: 5 minutes

Serving: 1

Ingredients:

- 1/2 ripe avocado, pitted and peeled
- 1 cup fresh spinach leaves
- 1/2 banana, peeled
- 1 cup unsweetened almond milk
- 1 tablespoon honey
- 1/2 teaspoon lemon juice
- 1 cup ice cubes

Instructions:

1. In your Nutribullet blender, combine the avocado, spinach, banana, almond milk, honey, lemon juice, and ice cubes.
2. Blend on high for about 30-45 seconds, or until the mixture is smooth and creamy, while tightly fastening the cover.
3. Pour the Avocado Spinach Dream into a glass, then enjoy.

KIWI KALE CRUSH

Preparation Time: 5 minutes

Cook Time: N/A

Serving: 1

Ingredients:

- 2 kiwis, peeled and sliced
- 1 cup kale leaves, stemmed
- 1/2 cup pineapple chunks
- 1/2 banana, peeled
- 1/2 cup coconut water
- 1 teaspoon chia seeds (optional)
- 1 cup ice cubes

Instructions:

1. In your Nutribullet blender, combine the kiwis, kale, pineapple, banana, coconut water, chia seeds (if using), and ice cubes.
2. Lock the lid of the blender and blend the mixture on high for 45 to 60 seconds or until it is smooth and vivid.
3. Pour the Kiwi Kale Crush into a glass, then sip it.
4. For the remaining recipes, use the same approach, modifying the ingredients and directions as necessary. Ary

MANGO SPINACH SUNRISE

Preparation Time: 5 minutes

Cook Time: N/A

Serving: 1

Ingredients:

- 1/2 cup mango chunks
- 1 cup fresh spinach leaves
- 1/2 cup Greek yogurt
- 1 tablespoon honey
- 1/2 teaspoon grated ginger
- 1 cup ice cubes

Instructions:

1. In your Nutribullet blender, combine the mango, spinach, Greek yogurt, honey, ginger, and ice cubes.
2. It normally takes 45 to 60 seconds to blend on high with the lid securely on until the mixture is smooth and sunny.
3. Enjoy the Mango Spinach Sunrise after pouring ig into a glass.

GREEN DETOX ELIXIR

Preparation Time: 5 minutes

Cook Time: N/A

Serving: 1

Ingredients:

- 1 cup kale leaves, stems removed
- 1/2 cucumber, peeled and sliced
- 1/2 lemon, peeled and seeded
- 1 green apple, cored and sliced
- 1 teaspoon fresh ginger, minced
- 1 cup water
- 1 cup ice cubes

Instructions:

1. In the Nutribullet blender, combine the kale leaves, cucumber, lemon, green apple, and ginger.
2. In addition to the other components, add water and ice cubes.
3. It should take 45 to 60 seconds to blend the mixture on high speed until it is smooth and bright green. Secure the cover of the blender.
4. Start your day with this revitalizing and cleansing beverage by pouring the Green Detox Elixir into a glass.

BLUEBERRY SPINACH FUSION

Preparation Time: 5 minutes

Cook Time: N/A

Serving: 1

Ingredients:

- 1 cup baby spinach leaves
- 1/2 cup blueberries (fresh or frozen)
- 1/2 banana
- 1/2 cup Greek yogurt
- 1 tablespoon honey
- 1/2 cup almond milk
- 1 cup ice cubes

Instructions:

1. In the Nutribullet blender, combine the baby spinach leaves, blueberries, banana, Greek yogurt, honey, and almond milk.
2. Over the other ingredients, add the ice cubes.
3. Secure the cover of the blender, then blend the mixture on high for 45 to 60 seconds or until it is smooth and has a lovely purple tint.
4. Enjoy the sweet and tangy tastes of the Blueberry Spinach Fusion in a glass after pouring it.

PINEAPPLE SPINACH SPLASH

Preparation Time: 5 minutes

Cook Time: N/A

Serving: 1

Ingredients:

- 1 cup fresh spinach leaves
- 1/2 cup pineapple chunks
- 1/2 banana
- 1/4 cup coconut milk
- 1/4 cup orange juice
- 1/2 teaspoon grated coconut (optional)
- 1 cup ice cubes

Instructions:

1. Fresh spinach leaves, pineapple chunks, bananas, grated coconut (if used), coconut milk, and orange juice should all be added to the Nutribullet mixer.
2. The ice cubes should be added on top of the other components.
3. The liquid should be smooth and tropical after about 45–60 seconds of high-speed blending. Secure the blender top.
4. Enjoy a taste of the islands by pouring the Pineapple Spinach Splash into a glass.

PEACHY GREEN POWER

Preparation Time: 5 minutes

Cook Time: N/A

Serving: 1

Ingredients:

- 1 cup baby spinach leaves
- 1 peach, pitted and sliced
- 1/2 cup Greek yogurt
- 1 tablespoon honey
- 1/2 cup almond milk
- 1 cup ice cubes

Instructions:

1. The Nutribullet blender should be filled with baby spinach leaves, peach slices, Greek yogurt, honey, almond milk, and ice cubes.
2. When the liquid is smooth and has a gorgeous peachy tint, often after approximately 45 to 60 seconds of blending on high, lock the blender lid.
3. After pouring a glass of Peachy Green Power, you may savor its luscious, fruity flavor.

COCONUT KALE CREAM

Preparation Time: 5 minutes

Cook Time: N/A

Serving: 1

Ingredients:

- 1 cup kale leaves, stems removed
- 1/2 cup coconut milk
- 1/2 banana
- 1/4 cup unsweetened shredded coconut
- 1 tablespoon honey
- 1/2 cup ice cubes

Instructions:

1. In the Nutribullet blender, combine the kale leaves, coconut milk, banana, coconut shreds, honey, and ice cubes.
2. Affix the cover to the blender, then blend the ingredients on high for 45 to 60 seconds or until the drink is smooth and flavorful of tropical coconut.
3. Enjoy the creamy and nourishing concoction by pouring the Coconut Kale Cream into a glass.

RASPBERRY SPINACH SWIRL

Preparation Time: 5 minutes

Cook Time: N/A

Serving: 1

Ingredients:

- 1 cup fresh spinach leaves
- 1/2 cup raspberries (fresh or frozen)
- 1/2 banana
- 1/2 cup Greek yogurt
- 1 tablespoon honey
- 1/2 cup almond milk
- 1 cup ice cubes

Instructions:

1. In the Nutribullet blender, combine the fresh spinach leaves, raspberries, banana, Greek yogurt, honey, almond milk, and ice cubes.
2. Closing the blender's cover, blend the ingredients for 45-60 seconds or until they're completely combined and a lovely pink color.
3. Enjoy the sweet and tangy mix of the Raspberry Spinach Swirl after pouring it into a glass.

APPLE SPINACH SPECTACULAR

Preparation Time: 5 minutes

Cook Time: N/A

Serving: 1

Ingredients:

- 1 cup fresh spinach leaves
- 1 apple, cored and sliced
- 1/2 cup Greek yogurt
- 1 tablespoon honey
- 1/2 teaspoon ground cinnamon
- 1/2 cup almond milk
- 1 cup ice cubes

Instructions:

1. In the Nutribullet blender, combine the fresh spinach leaves, apple slices, Greek yogurt, honey, cinnamon, almond milk, and ice cubes.
2. For generally between 45 and 60 seconds, lock the lid of the blender and blend the mixture on high until it is smooth and smells comfortingly of apple and cinnamon.
3. Pour a glass of the Apple Spinach Spectacular and savor this wholesome concoction.

GREEN TEA INFUSION

Preparation Time: 5 minutes

Cook Time: N/A

Serving: 1

Ingredients:

- 1 green tea bag
- 1 cup hot water
- 1 cup spinach leaves
- 1/2 cucumber, peeled and sliced
- 1/2 lemon, juiced
- 1 tablespoon honey (optional)
- 1 cup ice cubes

Instructions:

1. Allow the green tea bag to cool after steeping it in boiling water for 3 to 5 minutes.
2. To the Nutribullet blender, add the brewed green tea, spinach leaves, cucumber slices, lemon juice, honey (if preferred), and ice cubes.
3. Blend the mixture on high until it is smooth, then lock the cover of the mixer.
4. Enjoy this smoothie that is hydrating and full of antioxidants after adding the Green Tea Infusion to a glass.

PEAR AND SPINACH PERFECTION

Preparation Time: 5 minutes

Cook Time: N/A

Serving: 1

Ingredients:

- 1 ripe pear, cored and sliced
- 1 cup fresh spinach leaves
- 1/2 cup Greek yogurt
- 1 tablespoon honey
- 1/2 teaspoon vanilla extract
- 1/2 cup almond milk
- 1 cup ice cubes

Instructions:

1. In the Nutribullet blender, combine the pear slices, spinach leaves, Greek yogurt, honey, vanilla essence, almond milk, and ice cubes.
2. When the mixture is smooth and creamy, lock the lid of the mixer and continue blending on high.
3. Pour a glass of Pear and Spinach Perfection and enjoy the delicious blend of fruit and vegetables!

ALMOND SPINACH SUPREME

Preparation Time: 5 minutes

Cook Time: N/A

Serving: 1

Ingredients:

- 1 cup fresh spinach leaves
- 1/4 cup almonds
- 1 banana, peeled
- 1/2 cup unsweetened almond milk
- 1 tablespoon almond butter
- 1 teaspoon honey (optional)
- 1 cup ice cubes

Instructions:

1. In the Nutribullet blender, combine the fresh spinach leaves, almonds, banana, almond milk, almond butter, honey (if using), and ice cubes.
2. When the mixture is smooth, and the almonds are entirely mixed, lock the cover of the blender and continue blending on high.
3. Pour a glass of the Almond Spinach Supreme and savor this nutty and healthy smoothie!

LEMON LIME ZEST

Preparation Time: 5 minutes

Cook Time: N/A

Serving: 1

Ingredients:

- Juice of 1 lemon
- Juice of 1 lime
- 1 cup fresh spinach leaves
- 1/2 cup plain Greek yogurt

- 1 tablespoon honey
- 1/2 cup water
- 1 cup ice cubes

Instructions:

1. Put the juice from the lemons and limes in a bowl.
2. The Nutribullet blender should be filled with lemon and lime juice, fresh spinach leaves, Greek yogurt, honey, water, and ice cubes.
3. Close the lid of the blender and continue blending until the mixture is totally smooth and tangy.
4. Enjoy the citrusy taste explosion by adding the Lemon Lime Zest to a glass.

GINGER GREENS GALORE

Preparation Time: 5 minutes

Cook Time: N/A

Serving: 1

Ingredients:

- 1 cup fresh spinach leaves
- 1/2-inch piece of fresh ginger peeled
- 1/2 cucumber, peeled and sliced
- 1/2 lemon, juiced
- 1 teaspoon honey (optional)
- 1 cup water
- 1 cup ice cubes

Instructions:

1. In the Nutribullet blender, combine the fresh spinach leaves, ginger that has been finely diced, cucumber slices, lemon juice, honey (if using), and ice cubes.
2. Lock the lid of the blender and continue blending on high until the liquid is lively and smooth.
3. Enjoy the energizing flavor by pouring Ginger Greens Galore into a glass.

POMEGRANATE SPINACH SENSATION

Preparation Time: 5 minutes

Cook Time: N/A

Serving: 1

Ingredients:

- 1/2 cup pomegranate seeds (or 1/2 cup pomegranate juice)
- 1 cup fresh spinach leaves
- 1/2 banana, peeled
- 1/2 cup plain Greek yogurt
- 1 tablespoon honey
- 1/2 cup water
- 1 cup ice cubes

Instructions:

1. Pomegranate seeds should be juiced first in a juicer or separate press if you're using them.
2. In the Nutribullet blender, combine the pomegranate juice or seeds, banana, fresh spinach leaves, Greek yogurt, honey, water, and ice cubes.
3. When the liquid is smooth and loaded with antioxidants, lock the lid of the blender and continue blending on high.
4. Enjoy the delicious sweetness of the Pomegranate Spinach Sensation by pouring it into a glass.

ORANGE CREAMSICLE GREENS

Preparation Time: 5 minutes

Cook Time: N/A

Serving: 1

Ingredients:

- Juice of 2 oranges
- 1 cup fresh spinach leaves
- 1/2 cup vanilla Greek yogurt
- 1/2 banana, peeled
- 1 tablespoon honey
- 1/2 teaspoon vanilla extract
- 1 cup ice cubes

Instructions:

1. In a dish, squeeze the juice from the two oranges.
2. In the Nutribullet blender, combine the orange juice, fresh spinach leaves, vanilla Greek yogurt, banana, honey, vanilla essence, and ice cubes.
3. When the liquid is smooth and resembles a creamsicle, lock the cover of the mixer and continue blending on high.
4. The Orange Creamsicle Greens should be poured into a glass. Enjoy the creamy orange sweetness!

BERRY BLAST GREEN SMOOTHIE

Preparation Time: 5 minutes

Cook Time: N/A

Serving: 1

Ingredients:

- 1/2 cup mixed berries (strawberries, blueberries, raspberries)
- 1 cup fresh spinach leaves
- 1/2 banana, peeled
- 1/2 cup plain Greek yogurt
- 1 tablespoon honey
- 1/2 cup water
- 1 cup ice cubes

Instructions:

1. In the Nutribullet blender, combine the mixed berries, fresh spinach, banana, Greek yogurt, honey, water, and ice cubes.
2. When the liquid is smooth and full of fruity sweetness, lock the lid on the blender and continue blending on high.
3. Fill a glass with the Berry Blast Green Smoothie and savor the blast of berry flavor and a hint of greens!

WATERMELON WONDER GREENS

Preparation Time: 5 minutes

Cook Time: N/A

Serving: 1

Ingredients:

- 1 cup watermelon chunks
- 1 cup fresh spinach leaves
- 1/2 cucumber, peeled and sliced
- 1/2 lime, juiced
- 1 tablespoon honey
- 1/2 cup water
- 1 cup ice cubes

Instructions:

1. The Nutribullet blender should be filled with watermelon pieces, fresh spinach leaves, cucumber slices, lime juice, honey, water, and ice cubes.
2. When the liquid is smooth and delightfully moisturizing, lock the lid of the blender and continue blending on high.
3. Enjoy the cool, refreshing flavor of the Watermelon Wonder Greens after pouring some into a glass.

BANANA KALE KICKSTART

Preparation Time: 5 minutes

Cook Time: N/A

Serving: 1

Ingredients:

- 1 banana, peeled
- 1 cup fresh kale leaves, stems removed
- 1/2 cup plain Greek yogurt
- 1 tablespoon almond butter
- 1 teaspoon honey (optional)
- 1/2 cup almond milk
- 1 cup ice cubes

Instructions:

1. In the Nutribullet blender, combine the banana, fresh kale leaves, Greek yogurt, almond butter, honey (if using), almond milk, and ice cubes.
2. Lock the blender's cover and keep mixing on high until the mixture is vigorous and smooth.
3. The Banana Kale Kickstart should be poured into a glass. Enjoy this nutrient-rich green smoothie to jumpstart your day!

CRANBERRY SPINACH SURPRISE

Preparation Time: 5 minutes

Cook Time: 0 minutes

Serving: 1

Ingredients:

- 1 cup fresh spinach leaves
- 1/2 cup frozen cranberries
- 1/2 banana, peeled
- 1/2 cup unsweetened cranberry juice
- 1 tablespoon honey
- 1/2 cup ice cubes

Instructions:

1. In the Nutribullet blender, combine the fresh spinach leaves, frozen cranberries, banana, cranberry juice, honey, and ice cubes.
2. Lock the lid of the blender and blend the mixture on high for 45 to 60 seconds or until it is smooth and vivid.
3. Fill a glass with the Cranberry Spinach Surprise and savor the deliciously tangy acidity of this lovely green smoothie!

CARROT TOP GREENS

Preparation Time: 5 minutes

Cook Time: 0 minutes

Serving: 1

Ingredients:

- 1 cup carrot tops (greens only)
- 1/2 cup diced cucumber
- 1/2 apple, cored and sliced
- 1/2 lemon, juiced
- 1 cup coconut water
- 1/2 cup ice cubes

Instructions:

1. The Nutribullet blender should be filled with carrot tops, sliced cucumber, apple slices, lemon juice, coconut water, and ice cubes.
2. Attach the lid to the blender, then process the mixture for 30 to 45 seconds on high or until it is smooth and a striking shade of green.
3. Fill a glass with the Carrot Top Greens and enjoy the distinctive flavor of this nutrient-rich green smoothie!

SPIRULINA SUPERCHARGE

Preparation Time: 5 minutes

Cook Time: 0 minutes

Serving: 1

Ingredients:

- 1 teaspoon spirulina powder
- 1 banana, peeled
- 1/2 cup fresh spinach leaves
- 1/2 cup unsweetened almond milk
- 1 tablespoon honey
- 1/2 cup ice cubes

Instructions:

1. Put the banana, fresh spinach leaves, almond milk, honey, ice cubes, and spirulina powder in the Nutribullet mixer.
2. Affix the cover to the blender and blend the mixture on high for 45 to 60 seconds or until it is smooth and supercharged with green goodness.
3. Feel the energy boost from this brilliant green smoothie after adding the Spirulina Supercharge to a glass.

PAPAYA PARADISE GREENS

Preparation Time: 5 minutes

Cook Time: 0 minutes

Serving: 1

Ingredients:

- 1/2 cup diced papaya
- 1/2 cup fresh spinach leaves
- 1/2 cup pineapple chunks
- 1/2 cup coconut water
- 1/2 lime, juiced
- 1/2 cup ice cubes

Instructions:

1. In the Nutribullet blender, combine the chopped papaya, fresh spinach leaves, pineapple chunks, coconut water, lime juice, and ice cubes.
2. For generally 30 to 45 seconds, lock the blender top and blend the mixture on high until it is smooth and takes you to a papaya paradise.
3. Grab a glass, add some Papaya Paradise Greens, and enjoy the tropical tastes of this leafy treat!

STRAWBERRY SPINACH SERENADE

Preparation Time: 5 minutes

Cook Time: 0 minutes

Serving: 1

Ingredients:

- 1 cup fresh spinach leaves
- 1/2 cup frozen strawberries
- 1/2 banana, peeled
- 1/2 cup Greek yogurt
- 1 tablespoon honey
- 1/2 cup ice cubes

Instructions:

1. In the Nutribullet blender, combine the fresh spinach leaves, frozen strawberries, banana, Greek yogurt, honey, and ice cubes.
2. Secure the cover on the blender, then blend the contents on high for 45 to 60 seconds or until it is smooth and singing to your taste senses.
3. Enjoy the wonderful fusion of sweet and savory tastes by pouring the Strawberry Spinach Serenade into a glass.

ALOE VERA GREEN GLOW

Preparation Time: 5 minutes

Cook Time: 0 minutes

Serving: 1

Ingredients:

- 1/2 cup fresh aloe vera gel (peeled)
- 1 cup fresh spinach leaves
- 1/2 cucumber, diced
- 1/2 lemon, juiced
- 1 tablespoon honey
- 1/2 cup ice cubes

Instructions:

1. In the Nutribullet blender, combine the fresh aloe vera gel, fresh spinach leaves, chopped cucumber, lemon juice, honey, and ice cubes.
2. Close the blender's top and blend the ingredients for 30 to 45 seconds or until the mixture is completely smooth and glowing bright green.
3. Pour some Aloe Vera Green Glow into a glass, and savor its moisturizing and restorative qualities!

APRICOT ALMOND GREENS

Preparation Time: 5 minutes

Cook Time: 0 minutes

Serving: 1

Ingredients:

- 1/2 cup diced apricots
- 1/2 cup fresh spinach leaves
- 1/4 cup almonds
- 1/2 cup almond milk
- 1 tablespoon honey
- 1/2 teaspoon vanilla extract
- 1/2 cup ice cubes

Instructions:

1. In the Nutribullet blender, combine the chopped apricots, fresh spinach leaves, almonds, almond milk, honey, vanilla essence, and ice cubes.
2. Securing the top, blend on high for 45–60 seconds or until the mixture is smooth, allowing the apricots and almonds to stand out prominently in the mixture.
3. Fill a glass with the Apricot Almond Greens and savor the nutty flavor of this healthy smoothie!

CHIA SPINACH SMOOTHIE

Preparation Time: 5 minutes

Cook Time: 0 minutes

Serving: 1

Ingredients:

- 1 cup fresh spinach leaves
- 1/2 cup diced mango
- 1/2 banana, peeled
- 1 tablespoon chia seeds
- 1/2 cup unsweetened coconut milk
- 1 tablespoon honey
- 1/2 cup ice cubes

Instructions:

1. In the Nutribullet blender, combine the fresh spinach leaves, chopped mango, banana, chia seeds, coconut milk, honey, and ice cubes.
2. Chia seeds provide a delicious texture to the recipe, so secure the lid of the blender and blend on high for approximately 45 to 60 seconds or until the liquid is smooth.
3. Pour the Chia Spinach Smoothie into a glass and savor the tropical flavors and chia seed richness in this healthy treat!

TURMERIC TWIST GREENIE

Preparation Time: 5 minutes

Cook Time: 0 minutes

Serving: 1

Ingredients:

- 1 cup fresh spinach leaves
- 1/2 teaspoon ground turmeric
- 1/2 teaspoon ground ginger
- 1/2 cup pineapple chunks
- 1/2 cup coconut water
- 1 tablespoon honey
- 1/2 cup ice cubes

Instructions:

1. In the Nutribullet blender, combine the fresh spinach leaves, ground turmeric, ground ginger, pineapple chunks, coconut water, honey, and ice cubes.
2. Close the blender's top and blend the ingredients for 30 to 45 seconds or until the liquid is smooth and has a subtle spiciness from the turmeric and ginger.
3. Enjoy this anti-inflammatory Turmeric Twist Greenie in a glass after pouring it into your vessel.

BLUE SPIRULINA SPECTACLE

Preparation Time: 5 minutes

Cook Time: 0 minutes

Serving: 1

Ingredients:

- 1 teaspoon blue spirulina powder
- 1 banana, peeled
- 1/2 cup fresh spinach leaves
- 1/2 cup coconut milk
- 1 tablespoon honey
- 1/2 cup ice cubes

Instructions:

1. In the Nutribullet blender, combine the blue spirulina powder, banana, fresh spinach leaves, coconut milk, honey, and ice cubes.
2. Fasten the blender's cover and blend the ingredients on high for 45 to 60 seconds, or until the spirulina is completely incorporated and the mixture is a uniform blue.
3. Enjoy this aesthetically amazing and nutrient-dense blue-green smoothie by pouring the Blue Spirulina Spectacle into a glass.

HONEYDEW MELON MEDLEY

Preparation Time: 10 minutes

Cook Time: N/A

Serving: 2

Ingredients:

- 2 cups diced honeydew melon
- 1 cup cucumber, peeled and chopped
- 1/2 cup fresh mint leaves
- 1/2 lime, juiced
- 1 tablespoon honey
- 1/2 cup coconut water
- 1 cup ice cubes

Instructions:

1. In the Nutribullet blender, combine the diced honeydew melon, chopped cucumber, fresh mint leaves, lime juice, honey, coconut water, and ice cubes.
2. Closing the blender's cover, blend the ingredients for 45-60 seconds or until smooth and the flavors are evenly distributed.
3. This hydrated and delicious smoothie should be poured into glasses along with the Honeydew Melon Medley. Garnish with a mint leaf.

FIG AND SPINACH FUSION

Preparation Time: 7 minutes

Cook Time: N/A

Serving: 2

Ingredients:

- 1 cup fresh spinach leaves
- 1 cup ripe figs, stems removed and halved
- 1/2 cup Greek yogurt
- 1 tablespoon honey
- 1/4 cup almond milk
- 1/2 teaspoon vanilla extract
- 1 cup ice cubes

Instructions:

1. In the Nutribullet blender, combine the fresh spinach leaves, ripe figs, Greek yogurt, honey, almond milk, vanilla essence, and ice cubes.
2. When the mixture is smooth, and the vivid green and figgy purple have properly mixed, secure the lid of the blender and blend on high for 45 to 60 seconds.
3. Fill your glasses with the Fig and Spinach Fusion, and then taste this delicious and healthy smoothie!

WALNUT SPINACH SUPREME

Preparation Time: 8 minutes

Cook Time: N/A

Serving: 2

Ingredients:

- 2 cups fresh spinach leaves
- 1/2 cup walnuts
- 1 banana, peeled
- 1/2 cup plain Greek yogurt
- 1 tablespoon honey
- 1/2 teaspoon ground cinnamon
- 1 cup almond milk
- 1 cup ice cubes

Instructions:

1. In the Nutribullet blender, combine the fresh spinach leaves, walnuts, banana, Greek yogurt, honey, cinnamon powder, and ice cubes.
2. Affix the cover to the blender and run it on high for 45 to 60 seconds or until the mixture is smooth and the deep green color merges with the delicious nuts.
3. Pour the Walnut Spinach Supreme into glasses, garnish with a few crushed walnuts, and savor this creamy, nutrient-rich treat!

MATCHA GREEN ZEN

Preparation Time: 5 minutes

Cook Time: N/A

Serving: 1

Ingredients:

- 1 teaspoon matcha green tea powder
- 1 banana, peeled
- 1/2 cup unsweetened almond milk
- 1/2 cup Greek yogurt
- 1 tablespoon honey
- 1/4 teaspoon vanilla extract
- 1 cup ice cubes

Instructions:

1. Matcha green tea powder should be dissolved in a little boiling water and allowed to cool to room temperature.
2. Put the banana, Greek yogurt, honey, matcha powder that has been dissolved, almond milk, vanilla extract, and ice cubes into the Nutribullet mixer.
3. Secure the cover on the blender and run it on high for 45 to 60 seconds or until the mixture is smooth and evenly colored bright green.
4. Enjoy this smoothie that is high in antioxidants and induces tranquility by pouring the Matcha Green tranquility into a glass.

CLASSIC CHOCOLATE PROTEIN SHAKE

Preparation Time: 5 minutes

Cook Time: N/A

Serving: 1

Ingredients:

- 1 cup unsweetened almond milk
- 1 scoop of chocolate protein powder
- 1 tablespoon unsweetened cocoa powder
- 1/2 banana
- 1 tablespoon almond butter
- 1/2 teaspoon vanilla extract
- 1 cup ice cubes

Instructions:

1. To your Nutribullet blender, add the almond milk, chocolate protein powder, unsweetened cocoa powder, banana, almond butter, vanilla extract, and ice cubes.
2. Secure the cover on the blender, then blend the mixture on high for 30 to 45 seconds or until it is smooth and creamy.
3. Enjoy the rich, chocolaty pleasure of the Classic Chocolate Protein Shake by pouring it into a glass.

VANILLA ALMOND BLISS SHAKE

Preparation Time: 5 minutes

Cook Time: N/A

Serving: 1

Ingredients:

- 1 cup unsweetened almond milk
- 1 scoop vanilla protein powder
- 1 tablespoon almond butter
- 1/2 teaspoon honey
- 1/4 teaspoon almond extract
- 1/2 cup ice cubes

Instructions:

1. In your Nutribullet blender, combine the almond milk, vanilla protein powder, almond butter, honey, almond extract, and ice cubes.
2. Secure the cover on the blender, then mix the shake on high for 30 to 45 seconds or until it is smooth and creamy.
3. Enjoy the sweet and nutty flavor of the Vanilla Almond Bliss Shake by pouring it into a glass.

PEANUT BUTTER BANANA POWER SHAKE

Preparation Time: 5 minutes

Cook Time: N/A

Serving: 1

Ingredients:

- 1 cup unsweetened almond milk
- 1/2 banana
- 1 scoop protein powder (vanilla or chocolate)
- 2 tablespoons natural peanut butter
- 1 tablespoon honey
- 1/2 teaspoon cinnamon
- 1 cup ice cubes

Instructions:

1. In your Nutribullet blender, combine the almond milk, banana, protein powder, peanut butter, honey, cinnamon, and ice cubes.
2. For a normal 30-45 second period, secure the lid of the blender and blend the mixture on high until it is smooth and the flavors are evenly distributed.
3. Pour the protein-packed Peanut Butter Banana Power Shake into a glass, and savor the deliciousness!

STRAWBERRY FIELDS FOREVER PROTEIN SHAKE

Preparation Time: 5 minutes

Cook Time: N/A

Serving: 1

Ingredients:

- 1 cup unsweetened almond milk
- 1/2 cup fresh or frozen strawberries
- 1 scoop strawberry protein powder
- 1/2 banana
- 1 tablespoon honey
- 1/2 teaspoon vanilla extract
- 1 cup ice cubes

Instructions:

1. In your Nutribullet blender, combine the almond milk, strawberries, strawberry protein powder, banana, honey, vanilla extract, and ice cubes.
2. Secure the cover on the blender, then blend the mixture on high for 30 to 45 seconds or until the shake is smooth and the strawberry taste is discernible.
3. Fill a glass with the Strawberry Fields Forever Protein Shake and savor the delicious fruity protein treat!

BLUEBERRY BLAST PROTEIN SMOOTHIE

Preparation Time: 5 minutes

Cook Time: N/A

Serving: 1

Ingredients:

- 1 cup unsweetened almond milk
- 1/2 cup fresh or frozen blueberries
- 1 scoop vanilla protein powder
- 1/2 banana
- 1 tablespoon almond butter
- 1/2 teaspoon honey
- 1 cup ice cubes

Instructions:

1. Your Nutribullet blender should now include almond milk, blueberries, vanilla protein powder, banana, almond butter, honey, and ice cubes.
2. Secure the lid of the blender, then process the smoothie on high for 30 to 45 seconds or until it is creamy and the blueberries are well combined.
3. Fill a glass with the Blueberry Blast Protein Smoothie and enjoy the blast of berry flavor with a hint of almond!

MOCHA MADNESS PROTEIN SHAKE

Preparation Time: 5 minutes

Cook Time: N/A

Serving: 1

Ingredients:

- 1 cup brewed coffee, chilled
- 1/2 cup unsweetened almond milk
- 1 scoop of chocolate protein powder
- 1 tablespoon cocoa powder
- 1 tablespoon almond butter
- 1/2 ripe banana
- 1 cup ice cubes

Instructions:

1. In your Nutribullet blender, combine all the ingredients.
2. Blend till creamy and smooth.
3. Enjoy your Mocha Madness Protein Shake after pouring it into a glass!

TROPICAL PARADISE PROTEIN PUNCH

Preparation Time: 5 minutes

Cook Time: N/A

Serving: 1

Ingredients:

- 1/2 cup pineapple chunks
- 1/2 cup mango chunks
- 1/2 cup Greek yogurt
- 1 scoop vanilla protein powder
- 1/2 cup coconut water
- 1/2 cup ice cubes

Instructions:

1. Use your Nutribullet blender to combine all the ingredients.
2. Blend until ethereal and smooth.
3. Enjoy your Tropical Paradise Protein Punch after pouring it into a glass!

CINNAMON ROLL PROTEIN SHAKE

Preparation Time: 5 minutes

Cook Time: N/A

Serving: 1

Ingredients:

- 1 cup unsweetened almond milk
- 1 scoop vanilla protein powder
- 1/2 teaspoon ground cinnamon
- 1/4 teaspoon vanilla extract

- 1 tablespoon almond butter
- 1/2 cup rolled oats
- 1 tablespoon honey
- 1 cup ice cubes

Instructions:

1. In your Nutribullet blender, combine all the ingredients.
2. Until creamy and cinnamon-flavored, blend.
3. Enjoy your Cinnamon Roll Protein Shake after pouring it into a glass!

GREEN GODDESS PROTEIN SMOOTHIE

Preparation Time: 5 minutes

Cook Time: N/A

Serving: 1

Ingredients:

- 1 cup spinach leaves
- 1/2 ripe avocado
- 1/2 cup cucumber chunks
- 1 scoop vanilla protein powder
- 1/2 cup unsweetened almond milk
- 1 tablespoon honey
- 1/2 cup ice cubes

Instructions:

1. Use your Nutribullet blender to combine all the ingredients.
2. Blend until it's smooth and a bright green color.
3. Enjoy your Green Goddess Protein Smoothie after pouring it into a glass!

RASPBERRY CREAM DREAM SHAKE

Preparation Time: 5 minutes

Cook Time: N/A

Serving: 1

Ingredients:

- 1/2 cup raspberries
- 1/2 cup Greek yogurt
- 1 scoop vanilla protein powder
- 1/2 cup unsweetened almond milk
- 1 tablespoon honey
- 1/2 cup ice cubes

Instructions:

1. In your Nutribullet blender, combine all the ingredients.
2. Blend till the color is dreamy and pink.
3. Enjoy your Raspberry Cream Dream Shake after pouring it into a glass!

OATMEAL COOKIE PROTEIN SHAKE

Preparation Time: 5 minutes

Cook Time: N/A

Serving: 1

Ingredients:

- 1/2 cup rolled oats
- 1 scoop vanilla protein powder
- 1/2 teaspoon ground cinnamon
- 1/4 teaspoon vanilla extract
- 1 tablespoon almond butter
- 1/2 ripe banana
- 1 cup unsweetened almond milk
- 1 tablespoon honey
- 1 cup ice cubes

Instructions:

1. Use your Nutribullet blender to combine all the ingredients.
2. Blend until the consistency is like that of an oatmeal cookie.
3. Enjoy your Oatmeal Cookie Protein Shake after pouring it into a glass!

MANGO TANGO PROTEIN SMOOTHIE

Preparation Time: 5 minutes

Cook Time: N/A

Serving: 1

Ingredients:

- 1/2 cup mango chunks
- 1/2 cup Greek yogurt
- 1 scoop vanilla protein powder
- 1/2 cup unsweetened almond milk
- 1 tablespoon honey
- 1/2 cup ice cubes

Instructions:

1. In your Nutribullet blender, combine all the ingredients.
2. Blend ingredients until well-combined and flavorful of mango.
3. Enjoy your Mango Tango Protein Smoothie after pouring it into a glass!

COFFEE LOVER'S PROTEIN SHAKE

Preparation Time: 5 minutes

Cook Time: N/A

Serving: 1

Ingredients:

- 1 cup brewed coffee, chilled
- 1 scoop of chocolate protein powder
- 1/2 ripe banana
- 1 tablespoon almond butter
- 1/2 cup unsweetened almond milk
- 1 tablespoon honey
- 1 cup ice cubes

Instructions:

1. Use your Nutribullet blender to combine all the ingredients.
2. Blend till combined with coffee and smooth.
3. Enjoy your Coffee Lover's Protein Shake after pouring it into a glass!

SPINACH AND PINEAPPLE PROTEIN DELIGHT

Preparation Time: 5 minutes

Cook Time: N/A

Serving: 1

Ingredients:

- 1 cup spinach leaves
- 1/2 cup pineapple chunks
- 1 scoop vanilla protein powder
- 1/2 cup unsweetened almond milk
- 1/2 cup water
- 1 tablespoon honey
- 1 cup ice cubes

Instructions:

1. In your Nutribullet blender, combine all the ingredients.
2. Blend ingredients until they are well combined and smooth.
3. Enjoy your Spinach and Pineapple Protein Delight after pouring it into a glass!

CHOCOLATE PEANUT BUTTER CUP SHAKE

Preparation Time: 5 minutes

Cook Time: N/A

Serving: 1

Ingredients:

- 1 cup unsweetened almond milk
- 1 scoop of chocolate protein powder
- 1 tablespoon cocoa powder

- 2 tablespoons natural peanut butter
- 1/2 ripe banana
- 1 tablespoon honey
- 1 cup ice cubes

Instructions:

1. Use your Nutribullet blender to combine all the ingredients.
2. Blend until the consistency is creamy and resembles a chocolate peanut butter cup.
3. Enjoy your Chocolate Peanut Butter Cup Shake after pouring it into a glass!

BERRY BLAST PROTEIN FUSION

Preparation Time: 5 minutes

Cook Time: None

Serving: 1

Ingredients:

- 1 cup mixed berries (strawberries, blueberries, raspberries)
- 1/2 cup Greek yogurt
- 1 scoop of your favorite berry-flavored protein powder
- 1 tablespoon honey
- 1/2 cup unsweetened almond milk
- 1/2 cup ice cubes

Instructions:

1. Blend together in the Nutribullet the mixed berries, Greek yogurt, protein powder, honey, almond milk, and ice cubes.
2. Blend for 30-45 seconds, or until the sauce is creamy and smooth, with the cover securely on the blender.
3. Fill a glass with Berry Blast Protein Fusion and savor your protein-rich berry pleasure!

COCONUT MACAROON PROTEIN SHAKE

Preparation Time: 5 minutes

Cook Time: None

Serving: 1

Ingredients:

- 1/2 cup coconut milk
- 1/2 cup unsweetened almond milk
- 1 scoop vanilla protein powder
- 2 tablespoons shredded coconut (plus extra for garnish)
- 1/2 teaspoon almond extract
- 1/2 cup ice cubes

Instructions:

1. Your Nutribullet blender should be filled with ice cubes, coconut milk, almond milk, vanilla protein powder, shredded coconut, and almond extract.
2. It should take around 30 to 45 seconds to blend the ingredients until it is creamy and smooth. Lock the lid of the blender.
3. Enjoy the exotic sensations by pouring the Coconut Macaroon Protein Shake into a glass and adding some shredded coconut as a topping.

PEACH COBBLER PROTEIN SMOOTHIE

Preparation Time: 5 minutes

Cook Time: None

Serving: 1

Ingredients:

- 1 ripe peach, pitted and sliced
- 1/2 cup rolled oats
- 1 scoop vanilla protein powder
- 1/2 teaspoon ground cinnamon
- 1 cup unsweetened almond milk
- 1 tablespoon honey
- 1/2 cup ice cubes

Instructions:

1. In the Nutribullet blender, combine the ripe peach slices, rolled oats, vanilla protein powder, ground cinnamon, almond milk, honey, and ice cubes.
2. For generally 45 to 60 seconds, combine the contents in the blender with the cover until it is smooth and resembles a peach cobbler.
3. Fill a glass with the Peach Cobbler Protein Smoothie and savor the flavor of a beloved dessert in a healthy smoothie.

CHERRY ALMOND PROTEIN BLISS

Preparation Time: 5 minutes

Cook Time: N/A

Serving: 1

Ingredients:

- 1 cup unsweetened almond milk
- 1/2 cup frozen cherries
- 1/4 cup vanilla protein powder
- 2 tablespoons almond butter
- 1 tablespoon honey
- 1/2 teaspoon almond extract (optional)
- 1 cup ice cubes

Instructions:

1. In the Nutribullet blender, combine the ripe peach slices, rolled oats, vanilla protein powder, ground cinnamon, almond milk, honey, and ice cubes.
2. For generally 45 to 60 seconds, combine the contents in the blender with the cover until it is smooth and resembles a peach cobbler.
3. Fill a glass with the Peach Cobbler Protein Smoothie and savor the flavor of a beloved dessert in a healthy smoothie.

COOKIES AND CREAM PROTEIN SHAKE

Preparation Time: 5 minutes

Cook Time: N/A

Serving: 1

Ingredients:

- 1 cup unsweetened almond milk
- 1/2 cup low-fat Greek yogurt
- 1 scoop of cookies cream protein powder
- 2 chocolate sandwich cookies (e.g., Oreos)
- 1 tablespoon cocoa powder
- 1/2 teaspoon vanilla extract
- 1 cup ice cubes

Instructions:

1. In your Nutribullet blender, combine the following Ingredients: almond milk, Greek yogurt, cookies and cream protein powder, chocolate sandwich cookies, cocoa powder, vanilla extract, and ice cubes.
2. Lock the lid of the blender and blend the mixture on high for 45 to 60 seconds or until it is smooth and has the consistency of cookies and cream.
3. Enjoy the delectable flavor of cookies and cream in a protein-packed form by pouring the Cookies and Cream Protein Shake into a glass and, if preferred, garnishing with cookie crumbs.

PINA COLADA PROTEIN PARADISE

Preparation Time: 5 minutes

Cook Time: N/A

Serving: 1

Ingredients:

- 1 cup coconut milk
- 1/2 cup frozen pineapple chunks
- 1/4 cup vanilla protein powder
- 2 tablespoons unsweetened shredded coconut
- 1 tablespoon honey
- 1/2 teaspoon rum extract (optional)
- 1 cup ice cubes

Instructions:

1. In your NutriBullet, combine the coconut milk, frozen pineapple chunks, vanilla protein powder, shredded coconut, honey, and rum essence (if using).
2. Add the ice cubes on top of the remaining ingredients.
3. Secure the blender's lid and blend on high for 45 to 60 seconds or until the mixture is smooth and resembles a tropical Pina Colada.
4. Pour the Pina Colada Protein Paradise into a glass, top it off with some shredded coconut or a slice of pineapple, and savor it with an extra protein boost!

PUMPKIN PIE PROTEIN DELIGHT

Preparation Time: 5 minutes

Cook Time: N/A

Serving: 1

Ingredients:

- 1/2 cup canned pumpkin puree
- 1 cup unsweetened almond milk
- 1 scoop vanilla protein powder
- 1/2 teaspoon pumpkin pie spice
- 1 tablespoon honey or maple syrup
- 1/2 teaspoon vanilla extract
- 1/2 cup ice cubes
- Whipped cream

Instructions:

1. Pumpkin puree, almond milk, vanilla protein powder, pumpkin pie spice, honey or maple syrup (if used), vanilla extract, and ice cubes should all be put in the Nutribullet blender.
2. Secure the cover on the blender, then blend the mixture on high for 30 to 45 seconds or until it is smooth and creamy.
3. Fill a glass with the Pumpkin Pie Protein Delight.
4. You might choose to add some whipped cream and cinnamon on the top for the traditional pumpkin pie taste.
5. Enjoy your pumpkin delight with added protein!

MINT CHOCOLATE CHIP PROTEIN SHAKE

Preparation Time: 5 minutes

Cook Time: N/A

Serving: 1

Ingredients:

- 1 cup unsweetened almond milk
- 1 scoop of chocolate protein powder
- 1/4 teaspoon peppermint extract
- 1 tablespoon dark chocolate chips
- 1/2 banana, frozen
- 1/2 cup ice cubes
- Fresh mint leaves for garnish (optional)

Instructions:

1. Blend the almond milk, chocolate protein powder, peppermint extract, dark chocolate chips, frozen banana, and ice cubes in your Nutribullet blender.
2. For a normal 30-45 second period, lock the lid of the blender and process the ingredients on high until it is creamy and the chocolate chunks are completely absorbed.
3. Fill a glass with the Mint Chocolate Chip Protein Shake.
4. If preferred, add fresh mint leaves as a garnish for a cool touch.
5. Enjoy this shake's delicious mint and chocolate flavor combo while it's filled with protein!

BLACKBERRY VANILLA PROTEIN BLISS

Preparation Time: 5 minutes

Cook Time: N/A

Serving: 1

Ingredients:

- 1 cup unsweetened almond milk
- 1 scoop vanilla protein powder
- 1 cup fresh blackberries
- 1/2 banana
- 1/2 teaspoon vanilla extract
- 1/2 cup ice cubes
- Fresh blackberries for garnish (optional)

Instructions:

1. Blend the almond milk, vanilla protein powder, fresh blackberries, banana, vanilla essence, and ice cubes in your Nutribullet.
2. For a normal 30-45 second period, lock the lid of the blender and blend the mixture on high until it is smooth and the blackberries are completely incorporated.
3. Fill a glass with the Blackberry Vanilla Protein Bliss.
4. If preferred, add a few fresh blackberries as a garnish.
5. Enjoy this amazing blackberry and vanilla creation's protein and taste explosion!

LEMON BLUEBERRY PROTEIN BURST

Preparation Time: 5 minutes

Cook Time: N/A

Serving: 1

Ingredients:

- 1 cup unsweetened almond milk
- 1 scoop vanilla protein powder
- 1/2 cup fresh blueberries
- Zest of 1 lemon
- 1 tablespoon lemon juice
- 1/2 teaspoon vanilla extract
- 1/2 cup ice cubes
- Fresh blueberries and lemon slices for garnish

Instructions:

1. Blend the almond milk, vanilla protein powder, fresh blueberries, lemon juice, vanilla essence, and ice cubes in your Nutribullet.
2. For a normal 30-45 second period, lock the lid of the blender and blend the mixture on high until it is smooth and the blueberries are evenly distributed.
3. Fill a glass with the Lemon Blueberry Protein Burst.
4. You might want to add some fresh blueberries and a lemon slice as a decorative garnish.
5. Enjoy this protein-rich smoothie that is tangy and refreshing!

CARAMEL APPLE PIE PROTEIN SHAKE

Preparation Time: 5 minutes

Cook Time: N/A

Serving: 1

Ingredients:

- 1 medium apple, cored and diced
- 1 cup unsweetened almond milk
- 1 scoop vanilla protein powder
- 1 tablespoon caramel sauce
- 1/2 teaspoon ground cinnamon
- 1/4 teaspoon nutmeg
- 1 cup ice cubes

Instructions:

1. The Nutribullet blender should be filled with ice cubes, apple dice, almond milk, vanilla protein powder, caramel sauce, ground cinnamon, and nutmeg.
2. Secure the cover on the blender, then blend the mixture on high for 30 to 45 seconds or until it is smooth and creamy.
3. The Caramel Apple Pie Protein Shake should be poured into a glass, drizzled with more caramel sauce if desired, and enjoyed with a protein-rich snack.

KIWI KIWI KIWI PROTEIN SMOOTHIE

Preparation Time: 5 minutes

Cook Time: N/A

Serving: 1

Ingredients:

- 3 kiwis, peeled and chopped
- 1/2 cup Greek yogurt
- 1 scoop vanilla protein powder
- 1 tablespoon honey
- 1/2 cup water
- 1 cup ice cubes

Instructions:

1. The Nutribullet blender should be filled with chopped kiwis, Greek yogurt, honey, vanilla protein powder, water, and ice cubes.
2. Fasten the lid and turn the blender on high for 30 to 45 seconds, or until the liquid is completely smooth and the green color is fully shown.
3. Pour the protein-rich Kiwi Kiwi Kiwi Smoothie into a glass, and then savor this tasty delight.

SNICKERDOODLE PROTEIN SHAKE

Preparation Time: 5 minutes

Cook Time: N/A

Serving: 1

Ingredients:

- 1 cup unsweetened almond milk
- 1 scoop vanilla protein powder
- 1/2 teaspoon ground cinnamon
- 1/4 teaspoon ground nutmeg
- 1 tablespoon almond butter
- 1 tablespoon honey
- 1/2 teaspoon vanilla extract
- 1 cup ice cubes

Instructions:

1. In the Nutribullet blender, combine the almond milk, vanilla protein powder, almond butter, honey, ground cinnamon, ground nutmeg, and ice cubes.
2. Lock the blender's lid and blend the ingredients for 30 to 45 seconds or until they are silky smooth and flavored like snickerdoodles.
3. The snickerdoodle flavor of a snickerdoodle cookie is a pleasant addition to a protein-rich shake, so pour the Snickerdoodle Protein Shake into a glass and, if you want, top it with a touch of cinnamon.

WATERMELON MINT PROTEIN REFRESHER

Preparation Time: 5 minutes

Cook Time: N/A

Serving: 1

Ingredients:

- 2 cups fresh watermelon chunks
- 5-6 fresh mint leaves
- 1 scoop vanilla protein powder
- 1/2 lime, juiced
- 1/2 cup water
- 1 cup ice cubes

Instructions:

1. The Nutribullet blender should be filled with fresh watermelon chunks, mint leaves, vanilla protein powder, lime juice, water, and ice cubes.
2. For generally around 30-45 seconds, secure the blender cover and blend the contents on high until it is creamy and the tastes of watermelon and mint are detectable.
3. Enjoy this hydrated and protein-rich refreshment by pouring the watermelon mint protein refresher into a glass and adding a mint sprig as desired.

HAZELNUT MOCHA PROTEIN SHAKE

Preparation Time: 5 minutes

Cook Time: N/A

Serving: 1

Ingredients:

- 1 cup brewed coffee, cooled
- 1 scoop of chocolate protein powder
- 2 tablespoons hazelnut spread (e.g., Nutella)
- 1/2 cup unsweetened almond milk
- 1/4 teaspoon cocoa powder
- 1 cup ice cubes

Instructions:

1. In the Nutribullet blender, combine the cooled, freshly brewed coffee, chocolate protein powder, hazelnut spread, almond milk, cocoa powder, and ice cubes.
2. Secure the cover of the blender, then blend the mixture on high for 30 to 45 seconds or until it is smooth and flavorful of rich mocha.
3. Pour the protein-packed Hazelnut Mocha Protein Shake into a glass, top with a dash of cocoa powder if preferred, and savor the delicious pairing of hazelnut and mocha!

CRANBERRY ORANGE PROTEIN CRUSH

Preparation Time: 5 minutes

Cook Time: N/A

Serving: 1

Ingredients:

- 1/2 cup frozen cranberries
- 1 orange, peeled and segmented
- 1 scoop vanilla protein powder
- 1/2 cup Greek yogurt
- 1/2 cup unsweetened almond milk
- 1 tablespoon honey (optional)
- 1/2 cup ice cubes

Instructions:

1. Blend together in the Nutribullet the frozen cranberries, orange segments, protein powder, Greek yogurt, almond milk, and honey (if using).
2. On top of the other ingredients, sprinkle ice cubes.
3. Secure the cover on the blender, then mix for typically 30 to 45 seconds until it's smooth.
4. Enjoy your Cranberry Orange Protein Crush after pouring it into a glass!

BANANA NUT BREAD PROTEIN SMOOTHIE

Preparation Time: 5 minutes

Cook Time: N/A

Serving: 1

Ingredients:

- 1 ripe banana
- 1/4 cup rolled oats
- 1 scoop vanilla protein powder
- 1/2 teaspoon ground cinnamon

- 1 tablespoon almond butter
- 1 cup unsweetened almond milk
- 1/2 cup ice cubes

Instructions:

1. In the Nutribullet blender, combine the ripe banana, rolled oats, protein powder, ground cinnamon, almond butter, almond milk, and ice cubes.
2. Close the cover of the blender, then process for generally 45 to 60 seconds until the mixture is smooth.
3. Smoothie that tastes like banana bread and is good for you to drink.

BUTTER PECAN PROTEIN SHAKE

Preparation Time: 5 minutes

Cook Time: N/A

Serving: 1

Ingredients:

- 1/4 cup pecans
- 1 scoop vanilla protein powder
- 1 tablespoon almond butter
- 1/2 teaspoon maple syrup
- 1 cup unsweetened almond milk
- 1/2 teaspoon vanilla extract
- 1/2 cup ice cubes

Instructions:

1. In the Nutribullet blender, combine the pecans, protein powder, almond butter, maple syrup, almond milk, vanilla extract, and ice cubes.
2. Affix the cover to the blender, then blend for typically 45 to 60 seconds until the mixture is smooth and creamy.
3. Enjoy the creamy and nutty Butter Pecan Protein Shake after pouring it into a glass.

RASPBERRY LEMONADE PROTEIN QUENCHER

Preparation Time: 5 minutes

Cook Time: N/A

Serving: 1

Ingredients:

- 1/2 cup raspberries (fresh or frozen)
- Juice of 1 lemon
- 1 scoop vanilla protein powder
- 1 tablespoon honey
- 1 cup water
- 1/2 cup ice cubes

Instructions:

1. In the Nutribullet blender, combine raspberries, lemon juice, protein powder, honey, water, and ice cubes.
2. Blend until it is smooth and reviving, often for 30 to 45 seconds. Secure the blender cover.
3. Enjoy the tart Raspberry Lemonade Protein Quencher after pouring it into a glass!

PISTACHIO POWER PROTEIN SHAKE

Preparation Time: 5 minutes

Cook Time: N/A

Serving: 1

Ingredients:

- 1/4 cup shelled pistachios
- 1 scoop vanilla protein powder
- 1/2 ripe banana
- 1 cup unsweetened almond milk
- 1 tablespoon honey
- 1/2 teaspoon almond extract
- 1/2 cup ice cubes

Instructions:

1. In the Nutribullet blender, combine the pistachios, protein powder, ripe banana, almond milk, honey, almond extract, and ice cubes.
2. Affix the cover to the blender, then blend for 45 to 60 seconds or until the mixture is creamy and nutty.
3. Enjoy the distinctive flavor of the Pistachio Power Protein Shake after pouring it into a glass!

GUAVA PASSION PROTEIN FUSION

Preparation Time: 5 minutes

Cook Time: N/A

Serving: 1

Ingredients:

- 1/2 cup guava chunks (fresh or frozen)
- 1/2 cup passion fruit pulp
- 1 scoop vanilla protein powder
- 1/2 cup Greek yogurt
- 1/2 cup water
- 1/2 cup ice cubes

Instructions:

1. Greek yogurt, protein powder, guava chunks, passion fruit pulp, water, and ice cubes should all be added to the Nutribullet mixer.
2. Blend for typically 30 to 45 seconds with the lid on the blender until it is smooth and tropical-flavored.
3. Enjoy the delicious Guava Passion Protein Fusion after pouring it into a glass!

CUCUMBER MINT PROTEIN COOLER

Preparation Time: 5 minutes

Cook Time: N/A

Serving: 1

Ingredients:

- 1/2 cucumber, peeled and sliced
- 1/4 cup fresh mint leaves
- 1 scoop vanilla protein powder
- Juice of 1 lime
- 1 tablespoon honey
- 1 cup water
- 1/2 cup ice cubes

Instructions:

1. In the Nutribullet blender, combine cucumber slices, fresh mint leaves, protein powder, lime juice, honey, water, and ice cubes.
2. When the liquid is cooled and refreshing, blend for approximately 30 to 45 seconds after tightening the top.
3. Enjoy the energizing Cucumber Mint Protein Cooler after pouring it into a glass!

TIRAMISU PROTEIN SHAKE

Preparation Time: 5 minutes

Cook Time: N/A

Serving: 1

Ingredients:

- 1 shot of espresso (cooled)
- 1 scoop of chocolate protein powder
- 1 tablespoon unsweetened cocoa powder
- 1/2 teaspoon instant coffee granules (optional)

- 1/2 cup Greek yogurt
- 1/2 cup unsweetened almond milk
- 1/2 teaspoon vanilla extract
- 1/2 cup ice cubes

Instructions:

1. Prepare one shot of espresso and let it cool in a different container.
2. Put the ice cubes, Greek yogurt, almond milk, vanilla extract, chocolate protein powder, cocoa powder, instant coffee granules (if using), and cooled espresso into the Nutribullet blender.
3. Affix the cover to the blender and mix until creamy and decadent, typically for 45 to 60 seconds.
4. Pour the delicious Tiramisu Protein Shake into a glass, and sip it up!

APRICOT ALMOND PROTEIN ELIXIR

Preparation Time: 5 minutes

Cook Time: N/A

Serving: 1

Ingredients:

- 1/2 cup apricots (fresh or frozen)
- 1 scoop vanilla protein powder
- 1 tablespoon almond butter
- 1 cup unsweetened almond milk
- 1 tablespoon honey
- 1/2 teaspoon almond extract
- 1/2 cup ice cubes

Instructions:

1. In the Nutribullet blender, combine the apricots, protein powder, almond butter, almond milk, honey, almond extract, and ice cubes.
2. Lock the lid of the blender and blend for typically 45 to 60 seconds or until the mixture is smooth and decadent.
3. Enjoy the delicious Apricot Almond Protein Elixir after pouring it into a glass!

BLUEBERRY BASIL PROTEIN BLAST

Preparation Time: 5 minutes

Cook Time: N/A

Serving: 1

Ingredients:

- 1/2 cup blueberries (fresh or frozen)
- 4-5 fresh basil leaves
- 1 scoop vanilla protein powder
- 1/2 cup Greek yogurt
- 1/2 cup water
- 1 tablespoon honey
- 1/2 cup ice cubes

Instructions:

1. In the Nutribullet blender, combine blueberries, fresh basil leaves, protein powder, Greek yogurt, water, honey, and ice cubes.
2. Close the cover of the blender, then blend for typically 30 to 45 seconds until the mixture is smooth and flavorful to the brim.
3. Enjoy the distinctive flavor of the Blueberry Basil Protein Blast after pouring it into a glass!

TROPICAL PARADISE SMOOTHIE

Preparation Time: 5 minutes

Cook Time: N/A

Serving: 2

Ingredients:

- 1 cup frozen pineapple chunks
- 1/2 cup frozen mango chunks
- 1 ripe banana
- 1/2 cup Greek yogurt
- 1/2 cup coconut milk
- 1 tablespoon honey
- 1/2 cup ice cubes

Instructions:

1. In the Nutribullet blender, combine the frozen mango and pineapple pieces, ripe banana, Greek yogurt, coconut milk, honey, and ice cubes.
2. Secure the cover on the blender, then blend the mixture on high for 30 to 45 seconds or until it is smooth and creamy.
3. Enjoy this taste of the tropics by pouring the Tropical Paradise Smoothie into two glasses and garnishing with a pineapple or cherry slice.

BERRY BLAST BREAKFAST BOWL

Preparation Time: 10 minutes

Cook Time: N/A

Serving: 1

Ingredients:

- 1 cup mixed berries (strawberries, blueberries, raspberries)
- 1/2 cup Greek yogurt
- 1/4 cup rolled oats
- 1 tablespoon honey
- 1/2 banana, sliced
- 1 tablespoon sliced almonds (optional)
- Fresh berries and granola for topping (optional)

Instructions:

1. In the Nutribullet blender, combine the mixed berries, Greek yogurt, rolled oats, honey, and banana slices.
2. Blend on high for approximately 30 seconds, or until the mixture is thick and creamy, with the lid securely on the blender.
3. Fill a bowl with the Berry Blast Breakfast Bowl.
4. Add granola, sliced almonds, and fresh berries on top (if using).
5. Enjoy this filling and wholesome breakfast dish!

MANGO TANGO DELIGHT

Preparation Time: 5 minutes

Cook Time: N/A

Serving: 1

Ingredients:

- 1 cup frozen mango chunks
- 1/2 cup orange juice
- 1/4 cup Greek yogurt
- 1 tablespoon honey
- 1/2 teaspoon grated fresh ginger (optional)
- 1/2 cup ice cubes

Instructions:

1. In the Nutribullet blender, combine the frozen mango chunks, orange juice, Greek yogurt, honey, freshly grated ginger (if using), and ice cubes.
2. Affix the cover to the blender and blend the ingredients on high for 30 to 45 seconds or until it is silky smooth.
3. Take a sip of the Mango Tango Delight and enjoy the exotic tastes!

CITRUS SUNRISE SPLASH

Preparation Time: 5 minutes

Cook Time: N/A

Serving: 1

Ingredients:

- 1 orange, peeled and segmented
- 1/2 grapefruit, peeled and segmented
- 1/2 lemon, juiced
- 1/2 lime, juiced
- 1 cup water
- 1 tablespoon honey (optional)
- 1 cup ice cubes

Instructions:

1. In your Nutribullet blender, combine the orange and grapefruit segments, lemon and lime juices, water, and optional honey.
2. Over the other ingredients, add the ice cubes.
3. Close the cover of the blender, then blend for generally 30 to 45 seconds until the mixture is smooth.
4. Enjoy the reviving citrus taste explosion after pouring the Citrus Sunrise Splash into a glass!

PINEAPPLE PASSION PUNCH

Preparation Time: 5 minutes

Cook Time: N/A

Serving: 1

Ingredients:

- 1 cup fresh pineapple chunks
- 1/2 banana
- 1/2 cup coconut milk
- 1/2 cup orange juice
- 1 tablespoon honey (optional)
- 1 cup ice cubes

Instructions:

1. In your Nutribullet blender, combine the pineapple chunks, banana, coconut milk, orange juice, and honey (if using).
2. Over the other ingredients, add the ice cubes.
3. Affix the cover to the blender, then blend for typically 45 to 60 seconds until the mixture is creamy and smooth.
4. Take a sip of the Pineapple Passion Punch and picture yourself in a tropical paradise!

STRAWBERRY KIWI QUENCHER

Preparation Time: 5 minutes

Cook Time: N/A

Serving: 1

Ingredients:

- 1/2 cup strawberries, hulled
- 2 kiwis, peeled and sliced
- 1/2 cup Greek yogurt
- 1 tablespoon honey (optional)
- 1/2 cup water
- 1 cup ice cubes

Instructions:

1. In your Nutribullet blender, combine the strawberries, kiwis, Greek yogurt, honey (if using), water, and ice cubes.
2. It normally takes 45 to 60 seconds to properly integrate the strawberries and kiwis into the liquid after securing the cover of the blender.
3. In a glass, pour the Strawberry Kiwi Quencher, and savor the pleasant balance of sweet and sour flavors!

BLUEBERRY BLISS BOOST

Preparation Time: 5 minutes

Cook Time: N/A

Serving: 1

Ingredients:

- 1 cup blueberries
- 1/2 cup spinach leaves
- 1/2 banana
- 1/2 cup almond milk
- 1 tablespoon honey (optional)
- 1/4 teaspoon vanilla extract
- 1 cup ice cubes

Instructions:

1. In your Nutribullet blender, combine the blueberries, spinach leaves, banana, almond milk, honey (if using), vanilla extract, and ice cubes.
2. Secure the lid on the blender, then blend for 45 to 60 seconds or until the mixture is smooth and the bright blueberry color is visible.
3. Prepare for an antioxidant boost by pouring the Blueberry Bliss Boost into a glass.

PEACHY KEEN CREAMSICLE

Preparation Time: 5 minutes

Cook Time: N/A

Serving: 1

Ingredients:

- 1 cup fresh or frozen peach slices
- 1/2 cup Greek yogurt
- 1/2 cup orange juice
- 1 tablespoon honey (optional)
- 1/2 teaspoon vanilla extract
- 1 cup ice cubes

Instructions:

1. In your Nutribullet blender, combine the peach slices, Greek yogurt, orange juice, honey (if using), vanilla extract, and ice cubes.
2. Blend for 45 to 60 seconds, depending on your blender, until the mixture is smooth and the peach taste is prominent.
3. Enjoy the delicious blend of peach and creamy bliss by pouring the Peachy Keen Creamsicle into a glass.

WATERMELON MINT COOLER

Preparation Time: 5 minutes

Cook Time: N/A

Serving: 1

Ingredients:

- 1 cup fresh watermelon chunks
- 5-6 fresh mint leaves
- 1/2 lime, juiced
- 1/2 cup coconut water
- 1 tablespoon honey (optional)
- 1 cup ice cubes

Instructions:

1. In your Nutribullet blender, combine the watermelon chunks, fresh mint leaves, lime juice, coconut water, honey (if using), and ice cubes.
2. Blend the ingredients for typically 30 to 45 seconds, or until the liquid is smooth and the mint has given off its reviving taste.
3. Take a sip of the refreshing Watermelon Mint Cooler and enjoy the flavor of summer!

CHERRY BERRY BURST

Preparation Time: 5 minutes

Cook Time: N/A

Serving: 1

Ingredients:

- 1/2 cup frozen cherries
- 1/2 cup frozen mixed berries
- 1/2 cup unsweetened almond milk
- 1/2 cup Greek yogurt
- 1 tablespoon honey (optional)
- 1/2 teaspoon vanilla extract
- 1/2 cup ice cubes

Instructions:

1. In the Nutribullet blender, combine the frozen cherries, mixed berries, almond milk, Greek yogurt, honey (if using), vanilla extract, and ice cubes.
2. Secure the cover on the blender and run it on high for 45 to 60 seconds or until the mixture is smooth and the bright red color pops.
3. Enjoy the burst of delicious tastes by pouring the Cherry Berry Burst into a glass and garnishing it with a few fresh cherries or berries.

GREEN APPLE ZEST

Preparation Time: 5 minutes

Cook Time: N/A

Serving: 1

Ingredients:

- 1 green apple, cored and sliced
- 1 cup fresh spinach leaves
- 1/2 cup cucumber slices
- 1/2 lemon, juiced
- 1/2 cup water
- 1 tablespoon honey (optional)
- 1 cup ice cubes

Instructions:

1. The Nutribullet blender should be filled with green apple slices, fresh spinach leaves, cucumber slices, lemon juice, water, honey (if wanted), and ice cubes.
2. Blend the mixture on high for 45 to 60 seconds, or until it is smooth and a brilliant green color, with the lid securely on the blender.
3. Enjoy the zingy flavor of this green delight by pouring the Green Apple Zest into a glass and topping it with a tiny apple slice.

POMEGRANATE POWERHOUSE

Preparation Time: 5 minutes

Cook Time: N/A

Serving: 1

Ingredients:

- 1/2 cup pomegranate seeds
- 1/2 cup Greek yogurt
- 1/2 cup unsweetened pomegranate juice

- 1/2 cup fresh blueberries
- 1 tablespoon honey (optional)
- 1/2 teaspoon lemon zest
- 1 cup ice cubes

Instructions:

1. In the Nutribullet blender, combine the pomegranate seeds, Greek yogurt, pomegranate juice, fresh blueberries, honey (if wanted), lemon zest, and ice cubes.
2. When the liquid is smooth and has a deep magenta color, often after approximately 45 to 60 seconds of blending on high, lock the lid of the blender.
3. In a glass, pour the Pomegranate Powerhouse, top with a few more blueberries, and savor the delicious antioxidant treat!

BANANA BERRY BONANZA

Preparation Time: 5 minutes

Cook Time: N/A

Serving: 1

Ingredients:

- 1 banana, peeled
- 1/2 cup frozen strawberries
- 1/2 cup frozen blueberries
- 1/2 cup unsweetened almond milk
- 1/2 cup Greek yogurt
- 1 tablespoon honey (optional)
- 1/2 teaspoon cinnamon
- 1 cup ice cubes

Instructions:

1. In the Nutribullet blender, combine the banana, frozen strawberries, frozen blueberries, almond milk, Greek yogurt, honey (if using), cinnamon, and ice cubes.
2. Secure the cover of the blender, then blend the mixture on high for 45 to 60 seconds or until it is smooth and has a wonderful purple tint.
3. The Banana Berry Bonanza should be poured into a glass, dusted with a little bit of cinnamon, and then enjoyed!

GUAVA GUZZLER

Preparation Time: 5 minutes

Cook Time: N/A

Serving: 1

Ingredients:

- 1 guava, peeled and seeded
- 1/2 cup fresh pineapple chunks
- 1/2 cup coconut water
- 1/2 lime, juiced
- 1 tablespoon honey (optional)
- 1/2 cup ice cubes

Instructions:

1. In the Nutribullet blender, combine the peeled and seeded guava, fresh pineapple chunks, coconut water, lime juice, honey (if preferred), and ice cubes.
2. Affix the cover to the blender and run it on high for 45 to 60 seconds or until the mixture is smooth and bright orange.
3. In a glass, pour the Guava Guzzler, top with a little pineapple slice, and taste the unique aromas of this revitalizing concoction!

KIWI LIME KICKSTART

Preparation Time: 5 minutes

Cook Time: N/A

Serving: 1

Ingredients:

- 2 ripe kiwis, peeled and sliced
- Juice of 1 lime
- 1/2 cup spinach leaves
- 1/2 cup cucumber, sliced
- 1 tablespoon honey
- 1 cup ice cubes

Instructions:

1. In your Nutribullet blender, combine the kiwi slices, lime juice, spinach, cucumber, honey, and ice cubes.
2. Secure the cover on the blender, then blend the mixture on high for 30 to 45 seconds or until it is smooth and bright green.
3. In a glass, pour the Kiwi Lime Kickstart and savor the zesty, energizing flavor!

CRANBERRY CRUSH CLEANSER

Preparation Time: 5 minutes

Cook Time: N/A

Serving: 1

Ingredients:

- 1/2 cup cranberries, fresh or frozen
- 1 orange, peeled and segmented
- 1/2 cup Greek yogurt
- 1 tablespoon honey
- 1/4 cup water
- 1 cup ice cubes

Instructions:

1. In your Nutribullet blender, combine the cranberries, orange segments, Greek yogurt, honey, water, and ice cubes.
2. Fasten the blender's cover and blend the ingredients for 45 to 60 seconds on high speed or until completely smooth and bursting with cranberry flavor.
3. Enjoy the tart and tangy tastes that cleanse and refresh as you pour the Cranberry Crush Cleanser into a glass.

APRICOT ALMOND DREAM

Preparation Time: 5 minutes

Cook Time: N/A

Serving: 1

Ingredients:

- 2 ripe apricots, pitted and sliced
- 1/4 cup almonds, unsalted
- 1/2 cup almond milk
- 1 tablespoon honey
- 1/2 teaspoon almond extract
- 1 cup ice cubes

Instructions:

1. In your Nutribullet blender, combine the apricot slices, almonds, almond milk, honey, almond extract, and ice cubes.
2. Affix the cover to the blender and run it on high for 45 to 60 seconds or until the mixture is creamy and the almonds are well combined.
3. In a glass, pour the Apricot Almond Dream, and enjoy the nutty and fruity treat!

PAPAYA PARADISE POTION

Preparation Time: 5 minutes

Cook Time: N/A

Serving: 1

Ingredients:

- 1 cup ripe papaya, peeled, seeded, and cubed
- 1/2 cup coconut water
- 1/4 cup Greek yogurt
- 1 tablespoon honey
- 1/4 teaspoon lime zest
- 1/2 cup ice cubes

Instructions:

1. In the Nutribullet blender, combine the ripe papaya, coconut water, Greek yogurt, honey, lime zest, and ice cubes.
2. For around 30-45 seconds, or when the mixture is smooth and creamy, lock the cover of the mixer in place.
3. When you pour some of the papaya paradise elixir into a glass, garnish it with a lime wedge and some mint leaves, then take a sip, and your tastebuds will be whisked away to a lush tropical oasis.

COCONUT MANGO CREAM

Preparation Time: 5 minutes

Cook Time: N/A

Serving: 1

Ingredients:

- 1/2 cup ripe mango chunks
- 1/2 cup coconut milk
- 1/4 cup plain Greek yogurt
- 1 tablespoon honey
- 1/4 teaspoon vanilla extract
- 1/2 cup ice cubes

Instructions:

1. Put the ice cubes, coconut milk, Greek yogurt, honey, and vanilla essence in the Nutribullet mixer along with the pieces of ripe mango.
2. Affix the cover to the blender and blend the ingredients on high for 30 to 45 seconds or until it is silky smooth.
3. Enjoy the tropical tastes and creamy richness of the Coconut Mango Cream in a glass!

SPINACH AND PEAR ELIXIR

Preparation Time: 5 minutes

Cook Time: N/A

Serving: 1

Ingredients:

- 1 cup fresh spinach leaves
- 1 ripe pear, peeled, cored, and chopped
- 1/2 cup unsweetened almond milk
- 1 tablespoon honey
- 1/2 teaspoon fresh ginger, grated
- 1/2 cup ice cubes

Instructions:

1. In the Nutribullet blender, combine the fresh spinach leaves, ripe pear, almond milk, honey, fresh ginger, and ice cubes.
2. It normally takes between 45 and 60 seconds to combine the mixture at high speed until it is smooth and the bright green color is visible.
3. Enjoy the reviving and energetic elixir by pouring the spinach and pears into a glass.

ORANGE CREAMSICLE DELIGHT

Preparation Time: 5 minutes

Cook Time: N/A

Serving: 1

Ingredients:

- 1 large orange, peeled and segmented
- 1/2 cup Greek yogurt
- 1 tablespoon honey
- 1/4 teaspoon vanilla extract
- 1/2 cup ice cubes

Instructions:

1. In the Nutribullet blender, combine the orange segments, Greek yogurt, honey, vanilla essence, and ice cubes.
2. It normally takes between 30 and 45 seconds to combine the ingredients on high until it is creamy and resembles a creamsicle.
3. Fill a glass with Orange Creamsicle Delight and savor the deliciously sweet and tart flavor!

GRAPEFRUIT GINGER ZING

Preparation Time: 5 minutes

Cook Time: N/A

Serving: 1

Ingredients:

- 1/2 grapefruit, peeled and segmented
- 1/2 lemon, peeled and segmented
- 1/2-inch piece of fresh ginger, peeled
- 1 tablespoon honey
- 1/2 cup ice cubes

Instructions:

1. In the Nutribullet blender, combine the grapefruit, lemon, fresh ginger, honey, and ice cubes.
2. Affix the cover to the blender and puree the mixture on high for 30 to 45 seconds or until it is zesty and energizing.
3. Enjoy the zesty zing by pouring the Grapefruit Ginger Zing into a glass.

BLUEBERRY SPINACH SPECTACULAR

Preparation Time: 5 minutes

Cook Time: N/A

Serving: 1

Ingredients:

- 1/2 cup fresh blueberries
- 1 cup fresh spinach leaves
- 1/2 cup plain Greek yogurt
- 1 tablespoon honey
- 1/2 teaspoon vanilla extract
- 1/2 cup ice cubes

Instructions:

1. In the Nutribullet blender, combine the fresh blueberries, spinach leaves, Greek yogurt, honey, vanilla essence, and ice cubes.
2. Secure the cover on the blender and run it on high for 45 to 60 seconds or until the mixture is smooth and the bright purple color is visible.
3. Fill a glass with the Blueberry Spinach Spectacular and savor the antioxidant-rich treat!

PINEAPPLE COCONUT REFRESHER

Preparation Time: 5 minutes

Cook Time: N/A

Serving: 1

Ingredients:

- 1 cup fresh pineapple chunks
- 1/2 cup coconut water
- 1/4 cup coconut milk
- 1 tablespoon honey
- 1/2 cup ice cubes

Instructions:

1. The Nutribullet blender should be filled with fresh pineapple chunks, coconut water, coconut milk, honey, and ice cubes.
2. For roughly 30-45 seconds, lock the blender top and blend the ingredients on high until it is smooth and takes you to a tropical paradise.
3. Enjoy the unique flavors by pouring the Pineapple Coconut Refresher into a glass and topping it with a pineapple slice or cherry.

MIXED BERRY MEDLEY

Preparation Time: 5 minutes

Cook Time: N/A

Serving: 1

Ingredients:

- 1 cup mixed berries (strawberries, blueberries, raspberries)
- 1/2 cup Greek yogurt
- 1/2 cup unsweetened almond milk
- 1 tablespoon honey
- 1/2 teaspoon vanilla extract
- 1 cup ice cubes

Instructions:

1. In the Nutribullet blender, combine the mixed berries, Greek yogurt, almond milk, honey, vanilla extract, and ice cubes.
2. It should take between 45 and 60 seconds to smooth and creamy the mixture when blending on high with the lid securely on.
3. Enjoy the rush of berry sweetness after pouring the Mixed Berry Medley into a glass!

CUCUMBER MELON COOLER

Preparation Time: 5 minutes

Cook Time: N/A

Serving: 1

Ingredients:

- 1 cup cucumber, peeled and chopped
- 1 cup honeydew melon, cubed
- 1/4 cup fresh mint leaves
- 1 tablespoon lime juice
- 1/2 cup water
- 1 cup ice cubes

Instructions:

1. In the Nutribullet blender, combine the cucumber, honeydew melon, mint leaves, lime juice, water, and ice cubes.
2. Secure the cover on the blender, then blend the mixture on high for 45 to 60 seconds or until it is smooth and cold to the touch.
3. Fill a glass with the Cucumber Melon Cooler, top it off with a mint leaf, and savor this refreshing treat!

FIG AND HONEY HEAVEN

Preparation Time: 5 minutes

Cook Time: N/A

Serving: 1

Ingredients:

- 4 ripe figs, stems removed
- 1/2 cup Greek yogurt
- 1 tablespoon honey
- 1/4 teaspoon cinnamon
- 1/2 cup unsweetened almond milk
- 1 cup ice cubes

Instructions:

1. In the Nutribullet blender, combine the ripe figs, Greek yogurt, honey, cinnamon, almond milk, and ice cubes.
2. Lock the lid of the blender and blend the mixture on high for 45 to 60 seconds or until it is perfectly smooth and delicious.
3. Enjoy the sweet and creamy richness of the Fig and Honey Heaven in a glass!

KIWI STRAWBERRY SENSATION

Prep Time: 5 minutes

Cook Time: 0 minutes

Serving: 1

Ingredients:

- 2 kiwis, peeled and sliced
- 1 cup fresh strawberries, hulled
- 1/2 cup Greek yogurt
- 1 tablespoon honey
- 1/2 cup water
- 1 cup ice cubes

Instructions:

1. The Nutribullet blender should be filled with kiwis, strawberries, Greek yogurt, honey, water, and ice cubes.
2. Affix the cover to the blender and blend the mixture on high for 45 to 60 seconds or until it is creamy and delicious.
3. Pour some Kiwi Strawberry Sensation into a glass, then indulge in this cool treat!

LEMON LIME DETOX SPLASH

Prep Time: 5 minutes

Cook Time: 0 minutes

Serving: 1

Ingredients:

- Juice of 1 lemon
- Juice of 1 lime
- 1 tablespoon honey
- 1/2 teaspoon grated fresh ginger

- 1 cup water
- 1 cup ice cubes
- Fresh mint leaves for garnish (optional)

Instructions:

1. Juice from the lemon and lime should be squeezed into the Nutribullet.
2. Ice cubes, water, honey, and grated ginger are added.
3. Secure the lid on the blender and process the mixture for 30 to 45 seconds on high or until it is smooth and detoxifying.
4. Pour the Lemon Lime Detox Splash into a glass, add some fresh mint leaves as a garnish (if preferred), and savor this energizing concoction!

CHERRY VANILLA SWIRL

Prep Time: 5 minutes

Cook Time: 0 minutes

Serving: 1

Ingredients:

- 1 cup frozen cherries
- 1/2 cup plain Greek yogurt
- 1/2 teaspoon vanilla extract
- 1 tablespoon honey
- 1/2 cup unsweetened almond milk
- 1 cup ice cubes

Instructions:

1. Blend the frozen cherries, Greek yogurt, honey, almond milk, vanilla essence, and ice cubes in the Nutribullet.
2. It should take between 45 and 60 seconds to smooth out the mixture and create a beautiful cherry vanilla swirl while the blender is on high.
3. Fill a glass with the Cherry Vanilla Swirl and enjoy this sweet, creamy pleasure!

RASPBERRY CHIA DELIGHT

Preparation Time: 5 minutes

Cook Time: N/A

Serving: 2

Ingredients:

- 1 cup fresh or frozen raspberries
- 2 tablespoons chia seeds
- 1 banana, peeled
- 1 cup unsweetened almond milk
- 1 tablespoon honey or maple syrup
- 1 cup ice cubes

Instructions:

1. Blend the raspberries, chia seeds, banana, almond milk, and honey (if using) in your Nutribullet.
2. Over the other ingredients, add the ice cubes.
3. Blend until it's smooth and creamy, usually for 30 to 45 seconds. Secure the top of the blender.
4. Enjoy this wholesome and colorful smoothie by pouring the Raspberry Chia Delight into glasses and garnishing it with a few fresh raspberries or chia seeds.

CRAN-APPLE CINNAMON CRAVE

Preparation Time: 5 minutes

Cook Time: N/A

Serving: 2

Ingredients:

- 1 cup cranberries (fresh or frozen)
- 1 apple, cored and chopped
- 1 teaspoon ground cinnamon
- 1 cup unsweetened apple juice
- 1 cup ice cubes

Instructions:

1. In your Nutribullet blender, combine the cranberries, diced apple, cinnamon, and unsweetened apple juice.
2. Over the other ingredients, add the ice cubes.
3. Blend for generally 45–60 seconds, or until the mixture is smooth and the flavors are thoroughly incorporated, with the lid securely on the mixer.
4. Enjoy this delicious and cozy smoothie by pouring the Cran-Apple Cinnamon Crave into glasses and topping them with a bit of cinnamon if you want.

PAPAYA PINEAPPLE PARADISE

Preparation Time: 5 minutes

Cook Time: N/A

Serving: 2

Ingredients:

- 1 cup ripe papaya, diced
- 1 cup fresh pineapple chunks
- 1/2 cup coconut milk
- 1/2 cup orange juice
- 1 tablespoon honey or agave nectar
- 1 cup ice cubes

Instructions:

1. Papaya dice, pineapple chunks, coconut milk, orange juice, and honey (if used) should all be blended in your NutriBullet.
2. Over the other ingredients, add the ice cubes.
3. Blend for generally 30 to 45 seconds with the lid on the mixer or until the mixture is smooth and tropical-flavored.
4. Enjoy this unique and revitalizing smoothie by pouring the Papaya Pineapple Paradise into glasses and garnishing with a papaya or pineapple slice.

MANGO MINT MOJITO

Preparation Time: 5 minutes

Cook Time: N/A

Serving: 2

Ingredients:

- 1 ripe mango, peeled and pitted
- 1/4 cup fresh mint leaves
- 1 lime, juiced
- 1 tablespoon honey or agave nectar
- 1 cup coconut water
- 1 cup ice cubes

Instructions:

1. In your Nutribullet blender, combine the mango, fresh mint leaves, lime juice, honey (if using), and coconut water. Peel and pit the mango.
2. Over the other ingredients, add the ice cubes.
3. Blend the ingredients for generally 30 to 45 seconds, or until the drink is smooth and the mint lends a cool twist.
4. Before pouring the mango mint mojito into the glasses, garnish them with a lime wedge and a sprig of mint to enhance the tropical drink's flavor.

WATERMELON BASIL BLISS

Preparation Time: 5 minutes

Cook Time: N/A

Serving: 1

Ingredients:

- 1 cup fresh watermelon chunks
- 5-6 fresh basil leaves
- 1/2 cup cucumber, sliced
- 1/2 lime, juiced
- 1/2 cup coconut water
- 1 cup ice cubes

Instructions:

1. Put the coconut water, lime juice, cucumber slices, basil leaves, and watermelon pieces in the Nutribullet mixer.
2. Over the other ingredients, add the ice cubes.
3. Affix the cover to the blender and blend the mixture on high for 30 to 45 seconds or until it is smooth and reviving.
4. The ideal summertime treat should be poured into a glass, garnished with a basil leaf, and enjoyed!

GRAPEFRUIT GREEN GODDESS

Preparation Time: 5 minutes

Cook Time: N/A

Serving: 1

Ingredients:

- 1/2 grapefruit, peeled and segmented
- 1 cup fresh spinach leaves
- 1/2 cucumber, sliced

- 1/2 green apple, cored and chopped
- 1 tablespoon fresh mint leaves
- 1/2 cup coconut water
- 1 cup ice cubes

Instructions:

1. The Nutribullet blender should be filled with grapefruit segments, spinach leaves, cucumber slices, green apples, mint leaves, and coconut water.
2. Over the other ingredients, add the ice cubes.
3. Lock the lid of the blender and blend the mixture on high for 45 to 60 seconds or until it is smooth and full of vitamins.
4. Enjoy the hydrating and nutritious tastes by pouring the Grapefruit Green Goddess into a glass and adding a mint leaf as a garnish.

BERRY BANANA PROTEIN POWER

Preparation Time: 5 minutes

Cook Time: N/A

Serving: 1

Ingredients:

- 1/2 cup mixed berries (strawberries, blueberries, raspberries)
- 1 ripe banana
- 1/2 cup Greek yogurt
- 1 tablespoon honey
- 1/2 cup almond milk
- 1 scoop vanilla protein powder (optional)
- 1 cup ice cubes

Instructions:

1. Blend together in the Nutribullet the mixed berries, ripe banana, Greek yogurt, honey, almond milk, and protein powder (if using).
2. Over the other ingredients, add the ice cubes.
3. Lock the lid of the blender and blend the mixture on high for 45 to 60 seconds or until it is creamy and full of protein.
4. Drink some Berry Banana Protein Power, and then indulge in a wholesome and tasty post-workout snack!

PASSIONFRUIT PUNCH

Preparation Time: 5 minutes

Cook Time: N/A

Serving: 1

Ingredients:

- 2 ripe passionfruits, scooped out
- 1/2 cup pineapple chunks
- 1/2 cup orange juice
- 1/2 cup coconut milk
- 1 tablespoon honey
- 1 cup ice cubes

Instructions:

1. In the Nutribullet blender, combine the passionfruit pulp, pineapple pieces, orange juice, coconut milk, and honey.
2. Over the other ingredients, add the ice cubes.
3. Secure the cover of the blender, then blend the mixture on high for 45 to 60 seconds or until it is smooth and exploding with tropical flavors.
4. With this delicious and exotic smoothie, imagine yourself on a tropical island as you pour the Passionfruit Punch into a glass.

GREEN GODDESS POWER SMOOTHIE

Preparation Time: 5 minutes

Cook Time: N/A

Serving: 1

Ingredients:

- 1 cup fresh spinach leaves
- 1/2 cucumber, peeled and sliced
- 1/2 avocado, pitted and peeled
- 1/2 green apple, cored and sliced
- 1/2 lemon, juiced
- 1 cup coconut water
- 1 tablespoon honey
- 1 cup ice cubes

Instructions:

1. In the Nutribullet blender, combine the fresh spinach leaves, cucumber, avocado, green apple, lemon juice, coconut water, honey, and ice cubes.
2. The Green Goddess Power Smoothie should be poured into a glass, and you should enjoy its energizing flavor.

BERRY BLAST ENERGY ELIXIR

Preparation Time: 5 minutes

Cook Time: N/A

Serving: 1

Ingredients:

- 1/2 cup mixed berries (strawberries, blueberries, raspberries)
- 1/2 banana, peeled and sliced
- 1/2 cup Greek yogurt
- 1 tablespoon chia seeds
- 1 tablespoon honey
- 1/2 cup almond milk
- 1 cup ice cubes

Instructions:

1. Blend together in the Nutribullet the mixed berries, banana, Greek yogurt, chia seeds, honey, almond milk, and ice cubes.
2. Affix the cover to the blender and run it on high for 30 to 45 seconds or until the mixture is smooth and the bright cherry color is visible.
3. Enjoy the energy boost and antioxidant boost by pouring the Berry Blast Energy Elixir into a glass.

TROPICAL SUNRISE ENERGIZER

Preparation Time: 5 minutes

Cook Time: N/A

Serving: 1

Ingredients:

- 1/2 cup pineapple chunks
- 1/2 banana, peeled and sliced
- 1/2 orange, peeled and segmented
- 1/4 cup Greek yogurt
- 1 tablespoon honey
- 1/4 teaspoon grated ginger
- 1 cup coconut water
- 1 cup ice cubes

Instructions:

1. Put the Greek yogurt, honey, grated ginger, coconut water, orange segments, pineapple chunks, banana, and ice cubes into the Nutribullet mixer.
2. For about 45–60 seconds, lock the lid of the blender and blend the mixture on high until it is smooth and takes you to a tropical paradise.
3. Enjoy the tropical tastes that will boost your day by pouring the Tropical Sunrise Energizer into a glass.

CITRUS ZING ENERGY BOOSTER

Preparation Time: 5 minutes

Cook Time: N/A

Serving: 1

Ingredients:

- 1/2 grapefruit, peeled and segmented
- 1/2 lemon, peeled and segmented
- 1/2 orange, peeled and segmented
- 1 tablespoon honey
- 1/2 cup plain Greek yogurt
- 1/4 cup water
- 1 cup ice cubes

Instructions:

1. In the Nutribullet blender, combine the grapefruit, lemon, and orange segments, honey, plain Greek yogurt, water, and ice cubes.
2. Affix the cover to the blender and blend the mixture on high for 30 to 45 seconds or until it is smooth and lemony.
3. Feel the spicy surge of energy after pouring the Citrus Zing Energy Booster into a glass!

SUPERCHARGE SPINACH SMOOTHIE

Preparation Time: 5 minutes

Cook Time: N/A

Serving: 1

Ingredients:

- 1 cup fresh spinach leaves
- 1/2 ripe banana, peeled and sliced
- 1/2 cup mango chunks
- 1/2 cup pineapple chunks
- 1 tablespoon chia seeds
- 1 cup coconut water
- 1 cup ice cubes

Instructions:

1. Put the ripe banana, mango, pineapple, chia seeds, coconut water, and ice cubes in the Nutribullet mixer, along with the fresh spinach leaves.
2. Lock the lid of the blender and blend the mixture on high for 45 to 60 seconds or until it is smooth and vivid.
3. Enjoy the energy boost filled with vitamins and greens by pouring the Supercharge Spinach Smoothie into a glass.

ANTIOXIDANT VITALITY BLEND

Preparation Time: 5 minutes

Cook Time: N/A

Serving: 1

Ingredients:

- 1 cup mixed berries (blueberries, strawberries, raspberries)
- 1/2 cup spinach leaves
- 1/2 cup kale leaves
- 1/2 cup unsweetened pomegranate juice
- 1 tablespoon chia seeds
- 1/2 cup water
- 1 cup ice cubes

Instructions:

1. To your Nutribullet blender, add mixed berries, spinach, kale, pomegranate juice, chia seeds, and water.
2. On top of the other ingredients, sprinkle ice cubes.
3. Blend for generally 45 to 60 seconds or until the mixture is vivid and smooth. Secure the blender cover.
4. Take a drink of the Antioxidant Vitality Blend and enjoy the benefits of antioxidants throughout!

ALMOND JOY ENERGY SHAKE

Preparation Time: 5 minutes

Cook Time: N/A

Serving: 1

Ingredients:

- 1 ripe banana
- 2 tablespoons almond butter
- 2 tablespoons shredded coconut
- 1 tablespoon cocoa powder
- 1 cup unsweetened almond milk
- 1/2 teaspoon vanilla extract
- 1 cup ice cubes

Instructions:

1. In the Nutribullet blender, combine the banana, almond butter, coconut flakes, chocolate powder, almond milk, vanilla extract, and ice cubes.
2. It should take around 30-45 seconds to fully incorporate all the ingredients and make the drink creamy on high-speed blending.
3. Pour the Almond Joy Energy Shake into a glass, top with a little shredded coconut, and savor the delectable flavor of this treat for increased energy!

PINEAPPLE PASSION REVIVER

Preparation Time: 5 minutes

Cook Time: N/A

Serving: 1

Ingredients:

- 1 cup fresh pineapple chunks
- 1/2 cup fresh orange juice
- 1/2 cup Greek yogurt
- 1 tablespoon honey
- 1/2 teaspoon grated fresh ginger
- 1 cup ice cubes

Instructions:

1. In the Nutribullet blender, combine the fresh pineapple chunks, orange juice, Greek yogurt, honey, chopped ginger, and ice cubes.
2. Affix the cover to the blender and blend the mixture on high for 45 to 60 seconds or until it is smooth and flavorful of the tropics.
3. With each sip of the Pineapple Passion Reviver, you'll be whisked away to a warm paradise.

CUCUMBER MINT REFRESHMENT

Preparation Time: 5 minutes

Cook Time: N/A

Serving: 1

Ingredients:

- 1 cucumber, peeled and sliced
- 10 fresh mint leaves
- 1 cup water
- 1 cup ice cubes
- 1 teaspoon honey (optional)
- 1/2 lemon, juiced

Instructions:

1. In the Nutribullet blender, combine cucumber slices, mint leaves, water, ice cubes, and honey (if using).
2. Pour lemon juice over the remaining ingredients.
3. It should take around 30-45 seconds to blend the mixture at high speed until it is smooth and reviving. Secure the blender top.
4. Enjoy this energizing and hydrating beverage by pouring the cucumber mint refreshment into a glass and adding a mint sprig as a garnish.

BLUEBERRY BURST FUEL-UP

Preparation Time: 5 minutes

Cook Time: N/A

Serving: 1

Ingredients:

- 1 cup fresh or frozen blueberries
- 1/2 cup Greek yogurt
- 1/2 cup almond milk
- 1 tablespoon honey
- 1/2 teaspoon vanilla extract
- 1/2 cup ice cubes

Instructions:

1. Blend blueberries, Greek yogurt, almond milk, honey, vanilla essence, and ice cubes in the NutriBullet.
2. Lock the lid of the blender and blend the mixture on high for 45 to 60 seconds or until it is smooth and bursting with blueberry flavor.
3. Fill a glass with the Blueberry Burst Fuel-Up, then get ready to refuel with this tasty and healthy smoothie!

KALE KICKSTART SMOOTHIE

Preparation Time: 5 minutes

Cook Time: N/A

Serving: 1

Ingredients:

- 1 cup fresh kale leaves, stems removed
- 1/2 banana
- 1/2 cup pineapple chunks
- 1/2 cup coconut water
- 1 tablespoon chia seeds
- 1/2 cup ice cubes

Instructions:

1. In the Nutribullet blender, combine the kale leaves, banana, pineapple chunks, coconut water, chia seeds, and ice cubes.
2. Lock the lid of the blender and blend the mixture on high for 45 to 60 seconds or until it is smooth and full of nutrients.
3. Fill a glass with the Kale Kickstart Smoothie and get your day going with this nutrient-rich beverage!

GINGER SPICE ENERGY SHOT

Preparation Time: 5 minutes

Cook Time: N/A

Serving: 1

Ingredients:

- 1 small piece of fresh ginger peeled
- 1 lemon, juiced
- 1/2 teaspoon honey
- 1/4 teaspoon cayenne pepper (adjust to taste)
- 1/4 cup water
- Ice cubes (optional)

Instructions:

1. In the Nutribullet blender, combine the fresh ginger, lemon juice, honey, cayenne pepper, and water.
2. Add ice cubes if you like a chillier beverage.
3. It should take around 30-45 seconds to thoroughly integrate the ingredients and give the concoction a fiery kick when you secure the blender cover and blend on high.
4. Enjoy the energizing boost by pouring the Ginger Spice Energy Shot into a shot glass.

MANGO TANGO POWER PUNCH

Preparation Time: 5 minutes

Cook Time: N/A

Serving: 1

Ingredients:

- 1 cup fresh or frozen mango chunks
- 1/2 cup Greek yogurt
- 1/2 cup orange juice
- 1 tablespoon honey
- 1/2 teaspoon turmeric (optional for added health benefits)
- 1/2 cup ice cubes

Instructions:

1. In the Nutribullet mixer, combine the mango chunks, Greek yogurt, orange juice, honey, turmeric (if using), and ice cubes.
2. Secure the cover of the blender, then blend the mixture on high for 45 to 60 seconds or until it is smooth and exploding with tropical flavor.
3. Fill a glass with the Mango Tango Power Punch and enjoy the vivid smoothie to feel your energy soar!

CHOCOLATE PEANUT BUTTER BLISS

Preparation Time: 5 minutes

Cook Time: N/A

Serving: 1

Ingredients:

- 1 banana, peeled
- 2 tablespoons unsweetened cocoa powder
- 2 tablespoons natural peanut butter

- 1 cup unsweetened almond milk
- 1 tablespoon honey (optional)
- 1/2 teaspoon vanilla extract
- 1 cup ice cubes

Instructions:

1. In the Nutribullet blender, combine the banana, cocoa powder, peanut butter, almond milk, honey (if using), vanilla extract, and ice cubes.
2. Affix the cover to the blender and blend the mixture on high for 45 to 60 seconds or until it is smooth and decadently chocolaty.
3. Enjoy the delicious pairing of chocolate and peanut butter in a guilt-free pleasure by pouring the Chocolate Peanut Butter Bliss into a glass.

BEETROOT ENERGY SURGE

Preparation Time: 5 minutes

Cook Time: N/A

Serving: 1

Ingredients:

- 1 small beetroot, peeled and chopped
- 1 apple, cored and sliced
- 1 carrot, peeled and chopped
- 1/2 lemon, juiced
- 1/2 cup water
- 1/2 cup ice cubes

Instructions:

1. In the Nutribullet blender, combine the beetroot, apple, carrot, lemon juice, water, and ice cubes.
2. Lock the lid of the blender and blend the mixture on high for 45 to 60 seconds or until it is smooth and vivid.
3. Feel the natural energy rush from this nutrient-rich smoothie by pouring the Beetroot Energy rush into a glass.

COCONUT CREAM DELIGHT

Preparation Time: 5 minutes

Cook Time: N/A

Serving: 1

Ingredients:

- 1/2 cup coconut milk
- 1/2 cup Greek yogurt
- 1/2 ripe banana
- 1/4 cup shredded coconut
- 1 tablespoon honey
- 1/2 teaspoon vanilla extract
- 1 cup ice cubes

Instructions:

1. In your Nutribullet blender, combine the coconut milk, Greek yogurt, ripe banana, coconut shreds, honey, and vanilla essence.
2. Over the other ingredients, add the ice cubes.
3. In a blender fitted with a secure cover, combine all ingredients and process for 30–45 seconds or until smooth and coconutty.
4. Pour the Coconut Cream Delight into a glass, top with more shredded coconut if you'd like, and savor the delicious tropical flavor!

ORANGE CREAMSICLE VITALITY

Preparation Time: 5 minutes

Cook Time: N/A

Serving: 1

Ingredients:

- 1 large orange, peeled and segmented
- 1/2 cup Greek yogurt
- 1/2 cup almond milk

- 1 tablespoon honey
- 1/2 teaspoon vanilla extract
- 1 cup ice cubes

Instructions:

1. In your Nutribullet blender, combine the orange segments, Greek yogurt, almond milk, honey, and vanilla extract.
2. Over the other ingredients, add the ice cubes.
3. Secure the lid on the blender, then blend the contents on high for 30 to 45 seconds or until it is smooth and tastes like a traditional creamsicle.
4. Take a sip of the Orange Creamsicle Vitality while it's still cold, garnished with an orange slice.

ENERGIZING ESPRESSO FUSION

Preparation Time: 5 minutes

Cook Time: N/A

Serving: 1

Ingredients:

- 1 shot of espresso (cooled)
- 1/2 cup almond milk
- 1 ripe banana
- 1 tablespoon almond butter
- 1 teaspoon honey
- 1/2 teaspoon cocoa powder
- 1 cup ice cubes

Instructions:

1. Espresso should be made and let to cool.
2. In your Nutribullet blender, combine the cooled espresso, almond milk, ripe banana, almond butter, honey, chocolate powder, and ice cubes.
3. Fasten the blender's lid and blend the ingredients on high for 30 to 45 seconds or until they are completely smooth and full of life.
4. Fill a glass with the Energizing Espresso Fusion and enjoy a caffeine boost!

BANANA NUT PROTEIN BOOST

Preparation Time: 5 minutes

Cook Time: N/A

Serving: 1

Ingredients:

- 1 ripe banana, peeled
- 1/2 cup unsweetened almond milk
- 1/4 cup plain Greek yogurt
- 2 tablespoons natural almond butter
- 1 scoop vanilla protein powder
- 1/2 teaspoon cinnamon
- 1 tablespoon honey (optional)
- 1/2 cup ice cubes

Instructions:

1. In the Nutribullet blender, combine the banana, almond milk, Greek yogurt, almond butter, protein powder, cinnamon, and honey (if using).
2. Over the other ingredients, add the ice cubes.
3. Blend until it's smooth and creamy, generally for 30 to 45 seconds. Secure the cover.
4. Enjoy a tasty, protein-rich smoothie after adding the Banana Nut Protein Boost to a glass.

IMMUNE-BOOSTING CITRUS SPLASH

Preparation Time: 5 minutes

Cook Time: N/A

Serving: 1

Ingredients:

- 1 orange, peeled and segmented
- 1/2 lemon, peeled and seeded
- 1/2 lime, peeled and seeded
- 1/2 cup water
- 1 tablespoon honey (optional)
- 1/2 cup ice cubes

Instructions:

1. Put the lime, lemon, and orange segments in the Nutribullet mixer.
2. The citrus fruits should be topped with water and honey (if preferred).
3. Blend the mixture for about 30 seconds, with the cover on tightly, or until it is completely smooth.
4. Once the ice cubes are added, mix for an additional 15 to 20 seconds to thoroughly cool the smoothie.
5. Enjoy a pleasant and immune-boosting delight after pouring the Immune-Boosting Citrus Splash into a glass!

AVOCADO ALCHEMY ELIXIR

Preparation Time: 5 minutes

Cook Time: N/A

Serving: 1

Ingredients:

- 1 ripe avocado, peeled and pitted
- 1 cup unsweetened almond milk
- 1/2 teaspoon matcha green tea powder
- 1 tablespoon honey (optional)
- 1/2 teaspoon vanilla extract
- 1/2 cup ice cubes

Instructions:

1. In the Nutribullet blender, combine the ripe avocado, almond milk, matcha green tea powder, honey (if using), and vanilla essence.
2. Over the other ingredients, add the ice cubes.
3. Put the blender's cover on tight, and give it a good 45-60 seconds of blending time to get everything nice and smooth.
4. In a glass, pour the Avocado Alchemy Elixir, and have a distinctive and decadent green smoothie!

SUPERFOOD BERRY BURST

Preparation Time: 5 minutes

Cook Time: N/A

Serving: 1

Ingredients:

- 1 cup mixed berries (strawberries, blueberries, raspberries)
- 1/2 cup Greek yogurt
- 1 tablespoon chia seeds
- 1 tablespoon honey
- 1/2 cup unsweetened almond milk
- 1/2 teaspoon spirulina powder (optional)
- 1 cup ice cubes

Instructions:

1. In your Nutribullet blender, combine the mixed berries, Greek yogurt, chia seeds, honey, almond milk, ice cubes, and spirulina powder (if using).
2. Close the blender's cover and blend the ingredients for 30 to 45 seconds or until they are completely smooth and uniform in color.
3. The Superfood Berry Burst should be poured into a glass for you to enjoy this invigorating, antioxidant-rich smoothie.

KIWI LIME REJUVENATOR

Preparation Time: 5 minutes

Cook Time: N/A

Serving: 1

Ingredients:

- 2 ripe kiwis, peeled and sliced
- 1 lime, juiced
- 1/2 cup spinach leaves
- 1/2 cup coconut water
- 1 tablespoon agave nectar or honey
- 1 cup ice cubes

Instructions:

1. In your Nutribullet blender, combine the kiwis, lime juice, spinach leaves, coconut water, agave nectar or honey, and ice cubes.
2. Affix the cover to the blender and blend the mixture on high for 30 to 45 seconds or until it is smooth and reviving.
3. The Kiwi Lime Rejuvenator should be poured into a glass. Enjoy the zingy flavor of this healthy smoothie!

PROTEIN-PACKED PUMPKIN SPICE

Preparation Time: 5 minutes

Cook Time: N/A

Serving: 1

Ingredients:

- 1/2 cup canned pumpkin puree
- 1 cup unsweetened almond milk
- 1 scoop vanilla protein powder
- 1/2 teaspoon pumpkin pie spice
- 1 tablespoon maple syrup
- 1/2 teaspoon vanilla extract
- 1 cup ice cubes

Instructions:

1. In your Nutribullet blender, combine the canned pumpkin puree, almond milk, pumpkin pie spice, maple syrup, vanilla extract, and ice cubes.
2. Secure the cover on the blender, then blend the mixture on high for 30 to 45 seconds or until it is smooth and creamy.
3. The Protein-Packed Pumpkin Spice should be poured into a glass for a protein-rich smoothie that tastes like fall.

CHERRY ALMOND ENERGY LIFT

Preparation Time: 5 minutes

Cook Time: N/A

Serving: 1

Ingredients:

- 1 cup frozen cherries
- 1/4 cup almonds
- 1/2 cup plain Greek yogurt
- 1 tablespoon honey
- 1/2 cup water
- 1 cup ice cubes

Instructions:

1. Your Nutribullet blender should now include frozen cherries, almonds, Greek yogurt, honey, water, and ice cubes.
2. Lock the lid of the blender and blend the mixture on high for 45 to 60 seconds or until it is smooth and gives you an energy boost.
3. Place the Cherry Almond Energy Lift in a glass, then savor this wholesome smoothie.

GOJI BERRY ANTIOXIDANT CHARGER

Preparation Time: 5 minutes

Cook Time: N/A

Serving: 1

Ingredients:

- 1 cup unsweetened almond milk
- 1/2 cup frozen mixed berries
- 1/4 cup goji berries
- 1 tablespoon honey
- 1/2 teaspoon chia seeds
- 1/2 teaspoon flaxseed (ground)
- 1/2 teaspoon acai powder (optional)

Instructions:

1. To your Nutribullet blender, add almond milk, frozen berries, goji berries, honey (if using), chia seeds, flaxseed, and acai powder (if using).
2. Close the cover of the blender, then blend for generally 30 to 45 seconds until the mixture is smooth.
3. Enjoy the antioxidant boost by adding the Goji Berry Antioxidant Charger to a glass!

SWEET POTATO ENERGY EXPLOSION

Preparation Time: 5 minutes

Cook Time: N/A

Serving: 1

Ingredients:

- 1 small cooked sweet potato, peeled and cooled
- 1 cup unsalted salt
- 1 tablespoon almond butter
- 1 teaspoon honey or maple syrup
- 1/2 teaspoon cinnamon
- 1/4 teaspoon nutmeg
- 1/2 teaspoon vanilla extract

Instructions:

1. In your Nutribullet blender, combine the cooked sweet potato, coconut milk, almond butter, honey (if using), cinnamon, nutmeg, and vanilla extract.
2. Affix the cover to the blender, then blend for typically 45 to 60 seconds until the mixture is creamy and smooth.
3. The Sweet Potato Energy Explosion should be poured into a glass for consumption.

TURMERIC GOLD WELLNESS TONIC

Preparation Time: 5 minutes

Cook Time: N/A

Serving: 1

Ingredients:

- 1 cup coconut water
- 1/2 inch fresh turmeric root
- 1/2 inch fresh ginger root
- 1 tablespoon honey
- 1/2 lemon, juiced
- A pinch of black pepper

Instructions:

1. Your Nutribullet blender should now include coconut water, fresh turmeric, fresh ginger, honey, lemon juice, and a dash of black pepper.
2. Blend for generally 30 to 45 seconds, or until the drink is smooth and all the components are thoroughly incorporated, with the top securely on the blender.
3. Fill a glass with the Turmeric Gold Wellness Tonic and enjoy its immune-boostingand anti-inflammatory qualities!

CARROT GINGER VITALIZER

Preparation Time: 5 minutes

Cook Time: N/A

Serving: 1

Ingredients:

- 1 cup carrot juice
- 1/2 inch fresh ginger root
- 1/2 lemon, juiced

- 1 tablespoon honey (optional for sweetness)
- A pinch of ground cinnamon

Instructions:

1. Your Nutribullet blender should now include carrot juice, fresh ginger, lemon juice, honey (if using), and a small amount of ground cinnamon.
2. Blend for generally 30 to 45 seconds, or until the drink is smooth and all the components are thoroughly incorporated, with the top securely on the blender.
3. Enjoy this tangy and revitalizing beverage after pouring the Carrot Ginger Vitalizer into a glass.

RASPBERRY CHIA POWER POTION

Preparation Time: 5 minutes

Cook Time: N/A

Serving: 1

Ingredients:

- 1/2 cup frozen raspberries
- 1 cup
- tablespoon chia seeds
- 1 tablespoon honey
- 1/2 teaspoon vanilla extract

Instructions:

1. In your Nutribullet blender, combine frozen raspberries, almond milk, chia seeds, honey (if using), and vanilla extract.
2. When the liquid is smooth and the chia seeds have expanded, usually after approximately 45 to 60 seconds of blending, lock the cover of the blender in place.
3. Enjoy the energy boost and antioxidant boost by pouring the Raspberry Chia Power Potion into a glass!

WATERMELON WONDER REFRESHER

Preparation Time: 5 minutes

Cook Time: N/A

Serving: 1

Ingredients:

- 2 cups fresh watermelon chunks (seedless)
- 1/2 cucumber, peeled and sliced
- 1/2 lime, juiced
- A handful of fresh mint leaves
- 1 cup ice cubes

Instructions:

1. Your Nutribullet blender should be filled with fresh watermelon chunks, cucumber slices, lime juice, fresh mint leaves, and ice cubes.
2. Blend everything together for 30–45 seconds with the lid on or until the coffee aroma has fully diffused.
3. Fill a glass with the Watermelon Wonder Refresher, then sip on this hydrating and energizing beverage.

PAPAYA PARADISE FUEL

Preparation Time: 5 minutes

Cook Time: N/A

Serving: 1

Ingredients:

- 1 cup fresh papaya chunks (seeded and peeled)
- 1/2 cup Greek yogurt
- 1/2 banana, peeled
- 1 tablespoon honey
- 1/2 teaspoon lime zest
- 1/2 cup ice cubes

Instructions:

1. Blend together in your Nutribullet the fresh papaya chunks, Greek yogurt, banana, honey (if used), lime zest, and ice cubes.
2. Blend for generally 45 to 60 seconds or until the mixture is smooth and creamy. Secure the blender top.
3. Pour some Papaya Paradise Fuel into a glass, then savor this protein-rich and tropical concoction!

SPICY GREEN DETOX DYNAMO

Preparation Time: 5 minutes

Cook Time: N/A

Serving: 1

Ingredients:

- 1 cup kale leaves (stems removed)
- 1/2 cucumber, peeled and sliced
- 1/2 green apple, cored and sliced
- 1/2 lemon, juiced

- 1/2 inch fresh ginger root
- A pinch of cayenne pepper
- 1 cup coconut water
- 1/2 cup ice cubes

Instructions:

1. To your Nutribullet blender, add kale leaves, cucumber, green apple, lemon juice, fresh ginger, cayenne pepper, coconut water, and ice cubes.
2. Secure the blender's cover and mix on high for 45-60 seconds or until the sauce is entirely incorporated and has a smooth, spicy consistency.
3. Feel revitalized and energetic after adding the Spicy Green Detox Dynamo to a glass.

APRICOT ALMOND REVITALIZER

Preparation Time: 5 minutes

Cook Time: N/A

Serving: 1

Ingredients:

- 1/2 cup dried apricots (soaked in warm water for 10 minutes and drained)
- 1 cup unsweetened almond milk
- 1/4 cup plain Greek yogurt
- 1 tablespoon almond butter
- 1 tablespoon honey
- 1/2 teaspoon almond extract
- 1/2 cup ice cubes

Instructions:

1. Dried apricots that have been soaked and drained together with ice cubes, almond milk, Greek yogurt, almond butter, honey, and almond essence should be blended in a Nutribullet.
2. Blend for generally 45 to 60 seconds or until the mixture is smooth and creamy. Secure the blender top.
3. The natural sweetness and nutty tastes of the Apricot Almond Revitalizer may be enjoyed after pouring it into a glass.

MATCHA GREEN TEA BOOSTER

Preparation Time: 5 minutes

Cook Time: N/A

Serving: 1

Ingredients:

- 1 teaspoon matcha green tea powder
- 1 cup unsweetened almond milk
- 1/2 banana, peeled
- 1 tablespoon honey
- 1/2 teaspoon vanilla extract
- 1/2 cup ice cubes

Instructions:

1. Your Nutribullet blender should be filled with ice cubes, matcha green tea powder, almond milk, banana, honey (if using), and vanilla essence.
2. Affix the cover to the blender, then blend for generally 30 to 45 seconds or until the mixture is smooth and bright green.
3. Enjoy the matcha's powerful antioxidants and invigorating properties by pouring the Matcha Green Tea Booster into a glass.

MACA POWERHOUSE SMOOTHIE

Preparation Time: 5 minutes

Cook Time: N/A

Serving: 1

Ingredients:

- 1 banana, peeled and sliced
- 1 cup unsweetened almond milk
- 1 tablespoon maca powder
- 1 tablespoon almond butter
- 1 tablespoon honey
- 1/2 teaspoon ground cinnamon
- 1/4 teaspoon vanilla extract
- 1 cup ice cubes

Instructions:

1. In your Nutribullet blender, combine the banana, almond milk, maca powder, almond butter, honey, ground cinnamon, and vanilla extract.
2. Over the other ingredients, add the ice cubes.
3. Fasten the blender's lid and blend the ingredients for 45-60 seconds on high until completely smooth and creamy.
4. Pour a glass of the Maca Powerhouse Smoothie and savor this invigorating and healthy concoction!

POMEGRANATE PUNCH EUPHORIA

Preparation Time: 5 minutes

Cook Time: N/A

Serving: 1

Ingredients:

- 1/2 cup pomegranate seeds
- 1/2 cup plain Greek yogurt
- 1/2 cup unsweetened pomegranate juice
- 1/4 cup frozen raspberries
- 1 tablespoon honey
- 1/2 teaspoon lemon zest
- 1 cup ice cubes

Instructions:

1. In your Nutribullet blender, combine the pomegranate seeds, Greek yogurt, pomegranate juice, frozen raspberries, honey, and lemon zest.
2. Over the other ingredients, add the ice cubes.
3. It normally takes between 45 and 60 seconds to combine the mixture at high speed until it is smooth and the bright pink color is visible.
4. Fill a glass with Pomegranate Punch Euphoria and savor the delicious flavor and antioxidant goodness!

QUINOA BANANA PROTEIN SHAKE

Preparation Time: 5 minutes

Cook Time: N/A

Serving: 1

Ingredients:

- 1 banana, peeled and sliced
- 1/4 cup cooked quinoa, cooled
- 1 cup unsweetened almond milk
- 1 tablespoon almond butter
- 1 tablespoon honey
- 1/2 teaspoon ground cinnamon
- 1/4 teaspoon vanilla extract
- 1 cup ice cubes

Instructions:

1. In your Nutribullet blender, combine the banana, cooked quinoa, almond milk, almond butter, honey, ground cinnamon, and vanilla extract.
2. Over the other ingredients, add the ice cubes.
3. For generally around 45 to 60 seconds, combine the mixture on high speed until it is smooth, and the quinoa is completely integrated.
4. Enjoy this tasty and protein-rich smoothie by pouring the quinoa banana protein mix into a glass.

BLUE SPIRULINA BLISS

Preparation Time: 5 minutes

Cook Time: N/A

Serving: 1

Ingredients:

- 1 cup unsweetened almond milk
- 1 banana, peeled
- 1 teaspoon blue spirulina powder
- 1 tablespoon honey
- 1/2 teaspoon vanilla extract
- 1 cup ice cubes

Instructions:

1. In your Nutribullet blender, combine the almond milk, banana, blue spirulina powder, honey, and vanilla extract.
2. Over the other ingredients, add the ice cubes.
3. Secure the cover on the blender and run it on high for 45 to 60 seconds or until the mixture is smooth and the fascinating blue hue appears.
4. In a glass, pour the Blue Spirulina Bliss, and savor this colorful and nutrient-rich cocktail!

HONEYDEW MELON ENERGIZING SPLASH

Preparation Time: 5 minutes

Cook Time: N/A

Serving: 1

Ingredients:

- 1 cup honeydew melon chunks
- 1/2 cup cucumber, peeled and diced
- 1/2 cup unsweetened coconut water
- 1 tablespoon honey
- 1/2 teaspoon lime juice
- 1 cup ice cubes

Instructions:

1. In your Nutribullet blender, combine the honeydew melon pieces, sliced cucumber, coconut water, honey, and lime juice.
2. Over the other ingredients, add the ice cubes.
3. Secure the lid on the blender, then blend the mixture on high for 45 to 60 seconds or until it is smooth and a vibrant shade of invigorating green.
4. Enjoy this hydrating and energizing beverage by pouring the Honeydew Melon Energizing Splash into a glass!

CHAMOMILE CITRUS BLISS

Preparation Time: 5 minutes

Cook Time: N/A

Serving: 1

Ingredients:

- 1 chamomile tea bag
- 1 cup hot water
- 1/2 orange, peeled and segmented
- 1/2 lemon, peeled and segmented
- 1 tablespoon honey
- 1 cup ice cubes

Instructions:

1. The chamomile tea bag should be steeped in boiling water for 5 minutes. Give it time to reach room temperature.
2. In the Nutribullet blender, combine the brewed chamomile tea, orange and lemon segments, honey, and ice cubes.
3. Affix the cover to the blender and blend the mixture on high for 30 to 45 seconds or until it is smooth and reviving.
4. In a glass, pour the Chamomile Citrus Bliss, top with a citrus slice if you want, and savor the calming taste.

MINTY FRESH GREEN TEA

Preparation Time: 5 minutes

Cook Time: N/A

Serving: 1

Ingredients:

- 1 green tea bag
- 1 cup hot water
- 1/2 cucumber, peeled and sliced
-

- 5-6 fresh mint leaves
- 1 tablespoon honey
- 1 cup ice cubes

Instructions:

1. For three to four minutes, steep the green tea bag in boiling water. Give it time to reach room temperature.
2. In the Nutribullet blender, combine the brewed green tea, cucumber slices, fresh mint leaves, honey, and ice cubes.
3. The recommended blending time is 30 to 45 seconds on high or until the concoction is completely smooth and energetic.
4. In a tumbler, pour the Minty Fresh Green Tea, top with a mint sprig, and savor the refreshing flavor.

LAVENDER LEMONADE ELIXIR

Preparation Time: 5 minutes

Cook Time: N/A

Serving: 1

Ingredients:

- 1 cup fresh lemon juice
- 1 tablespoon culinary lavender buds
- 1/4 cup honey
- 1 cup ice cubes
- Lemon slices for garnish (optional)

Instructions:

1. The culinary lavender buds and two teaspoons of boiling water should be combined in a small bowl. After 5 minutes of steeping, strain to get the lavender buds out.
2. In the Nutribullet blender, combine the fresh lemon juice, honey, lavender-infused water, and ice cubes.
3. Affix the cover to the blender and blend the mixture on high for 30 to 45 seconds or until it is smooth and aromatic.
4. Enjoy the calming and fragrant elixir by pouring the lavender lemonade into a glass and adding lemon slices as desired.

GINGER TURMERIC SOOTHE

Preparation Time: 5 minutes

Cook Time: N/A

Serving: 1

Ingredients:

- 1 cup unsweetened almond milk
- 1/2 teaspoon ground turmeric
- 1/2 teaspoon grated fresh ginger
- 1 tablespoon honey
- 1/2 teaspoon ground cinnamon
- 1/2 teaspoon vanilla extract
- 1 cup ice cubes

Instructions:

1. In the Nutribullet blender, combine the unsweetened almond milk, ground turmeric, freshly grated ginger, honey, ground cinnamon, vanilla essence, and ice cubes.
2. Affix the cover to the blender and blend the mixture on high for 30 to 45 seconds or until it is smooth and soothing.
3. In a glass, pour the Ginger Turmeric Soothe, top with an additional pinch of ground cinnamon, and savor the comforting taste.

HIBISCUS BERRY BURST

Preparation Time: 5 minutes

Cook Time: N/A

Serving: 1

Ingredients:

- 1 cup hibiscus tea (brewed and cooled)
- 1/2 cup mixed berries
- 1/2 banana, peeled
- 1 tablespoon honey (optional)
- 1/2 cup ice cubes

Instructions:

1. Hibiscus tea should be made and allowed to cool to room temperature.
2. In the Nutribullet blender, combine the cooled hibiscus tea, mixed berries, banana, honey (if using), and ice cubes.
3. Secure the lid on the blender, then blend the mixture on high for 30 to 45 seconds or until it is smooth and vivid.
4. Enjoy the reviving blast of berry tastes by pouring the Hibiscus Berry blast into a glass.

ROSEMARY BLUEBERRY FUSION

Preparation Time: 5 minutes

Cook Time: N/A

Serving: 1

Ingredients:

- 1/2 cup fresh blueberries
- 1 sprig of fresh rosemary (leaves only)
- 1/2 cup plain Greek yogurt
- 1 tablespoon honey
- 1/2 cup water
- 1/2 cup ice cubes

Instructions:

1. In the Nutribullet blender, combine the fresh blueberries, rosemary, Greek yogurt, honey, water, and ice cubes.
2. Affix the cover to the blender and blend the mixture on high for 45 to 60 seconds or until it is aromatic and smooth.
3. Enjoy the distinctive fusion of rosemary and blueberry flavors by pouring the Rosemary Blueberry Fusion into a glass.

PEPPERMINT PATTY DELIGHT

Preparation Time: 5 minutes

Cook Time: N/A

Serving: 1

Ingredients:

- 1 cup unsweetened almond milk
- 1 tablespoon unsweetened cocoa powder
- 1 tablespoon honey
- 1/4 teaspoon peppermint extract
- 1/2 banana, peeled
- 1/2 cup ice cubes

Instructions:

1. In the Nutribullet blender, combine the banana, almond milk, chocolate powder, honey, peppermint essence, and ice cubes.
2. It normally takes between 30 and 45 seconds to smooth out the mixture and give it the delicious flavor of a peppermint patty when the blender is on high.
3. Enjoy the decadent but nutritious taste after pouring the peppermint patty delight into a glass.

CINNAMON APPLE SPICE

Preparation Time: 5 minutes

Cook Time: None

Serving: 1

Ingredients:

- 1 apple, cored and sliced
- 1/2 teaspoon ground cinnamon
- 1/2 cup unsweetened almond milk
- 1 tablespoon honey
- 1/2 teaspoon vanilla extract
- 1 cup ice cubes

Instructions:

1. In the Nutribullet blender, combine the apple slices, ground cinnamon, almond milk, honey, and vanilla essence.
2. Over the other ingredients, add the ice cubes.
3. Secure the cover on the blender and run it on high for 45 to 60 seconds or until the mixture is smooth and the air is filled with the soothing scent of cinnamon.
4. Pour the Cinnamon Apple Spice into a glass, garnish with a bit of cinnamon, and savor the comforting taste.

THYME AND HONEY INFUSION

Preparation Time: 5 minutes

Cook Time: None

Serving: 1

Ingredients:

- 1 cup water
- 1 sprig of fresh thyme
- 1 tablespoon honey
- 1/2 lemon, juiced
- 1 cup ice cubes

Instructions:

1. The water should be heated before being added to the Nutribullet.
2. Add the honey, lemon juice, and fresh thyme.
3. Let the mixture slightly cool.
4. After adding the ice, close the blender's cover.
5. Blend on high for generally 30 to 45 seconds or until the infusion is thoroughly incorporated and cold.
6. Place a thyme sprig on top of the Thyme and Honey Infusion, then sip the calming herbal infusion.

LEMON VERBENA ZEST

Preparation Time: 5 minutes

Cook Time: None

Serving: 1

Ingredients:

- 1 cup fresh lemon verbena leaves
- 1/2 lemon, juiced
- 1 tablespoon honey
- 1/2 cup water
- 1 cup ice cubes

Instructions:

1. In the Nutribullet blender, combine the fresh lemon verbena leaves, lemon juice, honey, and water.
2. Over the other ingredients, add the ice cubes.
3. Affix the cover to the blender, then blend the mixture on high for 45 to 60 seconds or until it is completely smooth.
4. Take a sip of your glass of Lemon Verbena Zest and enjoy the wonderful citrus notes.

FENNEL AND ORANGE CALM

Preparation Time: 5 minutes

Cook Time: None

Serving: 1

Ingredients:

- 1/2 orange, peeled and segmented
- 1/2 fennel bulb, thinly sliced
- 1/2 teaspoon honey
- 1/2 cup water
- 1 cup ice cubes

Instructions:

1. Lemon juice, honey, water, and fresh lemon verbena leaves should all be put in a NutriBullet mixer.
2. Add the ice cubes on top of the remaining ingredients.
3. Fix the lid to the blender, then process the combination for 45 to 60 seconds on high or until it reaches the desired smoothness.
4. Take a sip of your Lemon Verbena Zest beverage and savor the delicious citrus flavors.

EUCALYPTUS ECHINACEA BOOST

Preparation Time: 5 minutes

Cook Time: None

Serving: 1

Ingredients:

- 1 sprig of fresh eucalyptus leaves
- 1/2 teaspoon echinacea extract (liquid)
- 1/2 lemon, juiced
- 1 tablespoon honey
- 1 cup ice cubes

Instructions:

1. In the Nutribullet mixer, combine the fresh eucalyptus leaves, echinacea extract, lemon juice, honey, and ice cubes.
2. Lock the blender's lid and blend the ingredients for around 30 to 45 seconds or until silky and eucalyptus-scented.
3. Fill a glass with the Eucalyptus Echinacea Boost, and savor the immune-boosting benefits.

JASMINE GREEN TEA SERENITY

Preparation Time: 5 minutes

Cook Time: None

Serving: 1

Ingredients:

- 1 green tea bag (Jasmine or preferred variety)
- 1 cup hot water
- 1 tablespoon honey
- 1/2 lemon, juiced
- 1 cup ice cubes

Instructions:

1. Remove the green tea bag after steeping it in boiling water for three to five minutes.
2. Wait until the tea is at room temperature.
3. Blend the brewed green tea with the honey, lemon juice, ice cubes, and Nutribullet.
4. Affix the blender cover, then blend the ingredients on high for 30 to 45 seconds or until the mixture is cooled and well-flavored.
5. Pour some Jasmine Green Tea Serenity into a glass, and enjoy this calming combination for a moment of peace.

SAGE AND CRANBERRY QUENCHER

Preparation Time: 5 minutes

Cook Time: None

Serving: 1

Ingredients:

- 1/2 cup fresh sage leaves
- 1/2 cup cranberries (fresh or frozen)
- 1 tablespoon honey
- 1/2 cup water
- 1 cup ice cubes

Instructions:

1. In the Nutribullet blender, combine the fresh sage leaves, cranberries, honey, water, and ice cubes.
2. Fasten the blender's cover and blend the ingredients on high for 45 to 60 seconds or until the sage and cranberry flavors are well distributed.
3. Enjoy the tangy and herbal blend of the Sage and Cranberry Quencher in a glass.

FENNEL AND ORANGE CALM

Preparation Time: 5 minutes

Cook Time: N/A

Serving: 1

Ingredients:

- 1/2 fennel bulb, trimmed and sliced
- 1 orange, peeled and segmented
- 1/2 cup Greek yogurt
- 1 tablespoon honey
- 1/2 teaspoon ground cinnamon
- 1/4 cup water
- 1 cup ice cubes

Instructions:

1. In your Nutribullet blender, combine the sliced fennel, orange segments, Greek yogurt, honey, cinnamon powder, water, and ice cubes.
2. Fasten the blender's lid and blend the ingredients for 45-60 seconds on high until completely smooth and creamy.
3. Enjoy the calming and revitalizing tastes of the Fennel and Orange Calm smoothie by pouring it into a glass.

EUCALYPTUS ECHINACEA BOOST

Preparation Time: 5 minutes

Cook Time: N/A

Serving: 1

Ingredients:

- 1 cup fresh spinach leaves
- 1/2 cup pineapple chunks
- 1/2 cup orange juice
- 1/2 teaspoon eucalyptus oil (food grade)
- 1 teaspoon echinacea extract (alcohol-free)
- 1/4 cup water
- 1 cup ice cubes

Instructions:

1. In your Nutribullet blender, combine the fresh spinach leaves, pineapple chunks, orange juice, eucalyptus oil, echinacea extract, water, and ice cubes.
2. Affix the cover to the blender and blend the mixture on high for 45 to 60 seconds or until it is smooth and energizing.
3. Pour a glass of the Eucalyptus Echinacea Boost and enjoy the immune-boosting and energizing properties of this special smoothie.

JASMINE GREEN TEA SERENITY

Preparation Time: 5 minutes

Cook Time: N/A

Serving: 1

Ingredients:

- 1 green tea bag (jasmine flavor)
- 1 cup hot water
- 1/2 cup cucumber, peeled and sliced
- 1/2 cup honeydew melon chunks
- 1 tablespoon honey
- 1/2 teaspoon fresh lemon juice
- 1 cup ice cubes

Instructions:

1. Remove the tea bag from the jasmine green tea and allow the tea to cool to room temperature after steeping it in hot water for 3 to 4 minutes.
2. After the tea has cooled, combine it with the ice cubes, honey, honeydew melon pieces, cucumber slices, fresh lemon juice, and Nutribullet mixer.
3. Affix the cover to the blender and blend the mixture on high for 45 to 60 seconds or until it is calm and smooth.
4. Enjoy the peaceful and revitalizing tastes of the Jasmine Green Tea Serenity in a glass.

SAGE AND CRANBERRY QUENCHER

Preparation Time: 5 minutes

Cook Time: N/A

Serving: 1

Ingredients:

- 1/2 cup fresh cranberries
- 4-5 fresh sage leaves
- 1/2 cup unsweetened cranberry juice
- 1/2 cup plain kefir or yogurt
- 1 tablespoon honey
- 1/4 cup water
- 1 cup ice cubes

Instructions:

1. In your Nutribullet blender, combine the fresh cranberries, sage leaves, cranberry juice, plain kefir or yogurt, honey, water, and ice cubes.
2. Fasten the lid of the blender and process the mixture on high for 45 to 60 seconds, or until it is smooth and the flavors of the cranberry and sage have combined.
3. Pour the Sage and Cranberry Quencher into a glass and enjoy this revitalizing smoothie's distinctive blend of acidity and earthiness.

LEMONGRASS GINGER ZEN

Preparation Time: 5 minutes

Cook Time: N/A

Serving: 1

Ingredients:

- 1 stalk of fresh lemongrass, chopped
- 1-inch piece of fresh ginger
- 1 cup coconut water
- 1 tablespoon honey
- 1/2 lime, juiced
- 1 cup ice cubes

Instructions:

1. The Nutribullet blender should be filled with chopped lemongrass, grated ginger, coconut water, honey, and lime juice.
2. Over the other ingredients, add the ice cubes.
3. Lock the lid of the blender and blend the mixture on high for 45 to 60 seconds or until it is smooth and fragrant.
4. Enjoy the reviving and calming tastes of the Lemongrass Ginger Zen by pouring it into a glass.

RASPBERRY ROSE DELIGHT

Preparation Time: 5 minutes

Cook Time: N/A

Serving: 1

Ingredients:

- 1 cup fresh raspberries
- 1/2 cup rosewater
- 1/2 cup Greek yogurt
- 1 tablespoon honey
- 1/4 cup water
- 1 cup ice cubes

Instructions:

1. In the Nutribullet blender, combine the fresh raspberries, rosewater, Greek yogurt, honey, and water.
2. Over the other ingredients, add the ice cubes.
3. Secure the cover on the blender and run it on high for 45 to 60 seconds or until the mixture is smooth and a nice pink hue appears.
4. Pour some Raspberry Rose Delight into a glass and savor its delicious and romantic flavor.

LAVENDER VANILLA DREAM

Preparation Time: 5 minutes

Cook Time: N/A

Serving: 1

Ingredients:

- 1 teaspoon dried lavender buds
- 1/2 teaspoon vanilla extract
- 1 cup almond milk
- 1 tablespoon honey
- 1/4 cup rolled oats
- 1 cup ice cubes

Instructions:

1. Put the rolled oats, almond milk, honey, vanilla essence, and dried lavender buds in the Nutribullet blender.
2. Over the other ingredients, add the ice cubes.
3. After securing the top, blend the mixture for 45 to 60 seconds on high or until it is smooth and lavender-scented.
4. Enjoy the relaxing and aromatic scents of the Lavender Vanilla Dream after pouring it into a glass.

DANDELION DETOX ELIXIR

Preparation Time: 5 minutes

Cook Time: N/A

Serving: 1

Ingredients:

- 1 cup dandelion greens
- 1/2 cucumber, peeled and sliced
- 1/2 lemon, peeled and seeded
- 1/2 green apple, cored and sliced
- 1 tablespoon fresh mint leaves
- 1/2 cup water
- 1 cup ice cubes

Instructions:

1. The Nutribullet blender should be filled with dandelion greens, cucumber slices, peeled lemon, sliced green apple, and fresh mint leaves.
2. Over the other ingredients, add the ice cubes.
3. Lock the lid of the blender and blend the mixture on high for 45 to 60 seconds or until it is smooth and detoxifying.
4. Enjoy the purifying and energizing concoction by pouring the dandelion detox elixir into a glass.

STRAWBERRY BASIL BLISS

Preparation Time: 5 minutes

Cook Time: N/A

Serving: 1

Ingredients:

- 1 cup fresh strawberries, hulled
- 4-5 fresh basil leaves
- 1/2 cup coconut water
- 1 tablespoon honey
- 1/2 lime, juiced
- 1 cup ice cubes

Instructions:

1. Put the Nutribullet blender filled with fresh strawberries, basil leaves, coconut water, honey, and lime juice.
2. Over the other ingredients, add the ice cubes.
3. Lock the lid of the blender and blend the mixture on high for 45 to 60 seconds or until it is smooth and the sweet and herbal tastes are combined.
4. In a glass, pour the Strawberry Basil Bliss and savor the delicious and energizing flavor.

CARDAMOM CHAI INFUSION

Preparation Time: 5 minutes

Cook Time: N/A

Serving: 1

Ingredients:

- 1 black tea bag
- 1/2 teaspoon ground cardamom
- 1/2 teaspoon ground cinnamon
- 1/2 teaspoon ground cloves
- 1/2 teaspoon ground ginger
- 1 cup almond milk
- 1 tablespoon honey
- 1 cup ice cubes

Instructions:

1. In a cup of boiling water, steep the black tea bag for three to five minutes. Take out the teabag, then let it cool.
2. The Nutribullet blender should be filled with chilled black tea, ground cardamom, ground cinnamon, ground cloves, ground ginger, almond milk, honey, and ice cubes.
3. Affix the cover to the blender and blend the contents on high for 45 to 60 seconds or until it is smooth and smells like warm, comfortable tea.
4. Enjoy the fragrant and spicy Cardamom Chai Infusion by pouring it into a glass.

PINEAPPLE SAGE REFRESHER

Preparation Time: 5 minutes

Cook Time: N/A

Serving: 1

Ingredients:

- 1 cup fresh pineapple chunks
- 4-5 fresh sage leaves
- 1/2 cup coconut water
- 1/2 lime, juiced
- 1 tablespoon honey
- 1 cup ice cubes

Instructions:

1. Place the fresh pineapple chunks, sage leaves, coconut water, lime juice, honey, and ice cubes into the Nutribullet blender.
2. Secure the blender lid and blend on high until the mixture is smooth and the tropical pineapple flavor mingles with the herbal sage, typically for about 45-60 seconds.
3. Pour the Pineapple Sage Refresher into a glass, and enjoy the revitalizing and unique taste.

TURMERIC LEMONGRASS FUSION

Preparation Time: 5 minutes

Cook Time: N/A

Serving: 1

Ingredients:

- 1-inch piece of fresh turmeric
- 1 stalk of fresh lemongrass, chopped
- 1 cup coconut water
- 1 tablespoon honey
- 1/2 lemon, juiced
- 1 cup ice cubes

Instructions:

1. The Nutribullet blender should be filled with grated turmeric, chopped lemongrass, coconut water, honey, lemon juice, and ice cubes.
2. Affix the cover to the blender and run it on high for 45 to 60 seconds or until the mixture is smooth and flavorful.
3. Enjoy the spicy and citrusy blend of the Turmeric Lemongrass blend by pouring it into a glass.

BLUEBERRY LAVENDER LOVE

Preparation Time: 5 minutes

Cook Time: N/A

Serving: 1

Ingredients:

- 1/2 cup fresh blueberries
- 1 teaspoon dried lavender buds
- 1/2 cup Greek yogurt
- 1 tablespoon honey
- 1/4 cup water
- 1 cup ice cubes

Instructions:

1. Greek yogurt, honey, dried lavender buds, water, ice cubes, and fresh blueberries should all be added to the Nutribullet mixer.
2. Once the blender's cover is on tightly, blend the mixture for 45 to 60 seconds on high or until it is smooth and aromatic with lavender and blueberries.
3. Fill a glass with the Blueberry Lavender Love and savor the sweet and fragrant blend.

MINTY PINEAPPLE DELIGHT

Preparation Time: 5 minutes

Cook Time: N/A

Serving: 1

Ingredients:

- 1 cup fresh pineapple chunks
- 4-5 fresh mint leaves
- 1/2 cup coconut water
- 1/2 lime, juiced
- 1 tablespoon honey
- 1 cup ice cubes

Instructions:

1. In the Nutribullet blender, combine the fresh pineapple chunks, mint leaves, coconut water, lime juice, honey, and ice cubes.
2. Affix the top to the blender, then blend the ingredients on high for 45 to 60 seconds or until the tropical pineapple and revitalizing mint are harmoniously combined.
3. The refreshing and tropical flavor of the Minty Pineapple Delight may be enjoyed by pouring it into a glass.

ROSE PETAL RADIANCE

Preparation Time: 5 minutes

Cook Time: N/A

Serving: 1

Ingredients:

- 1 cup rose water
- 1/2 cup strawberries, hulled
- 1/4 cup fresh rose petals (organic, pesticide-free)
- 1 tablespoon honey
- 1/2 cup ice cubes

Instructions:

1. Blend the strawberries, fresh rose petals, rose water, honey, and ice cubes in a NutriBullet.
2. Secure the cover on the blender and run it on high for 45 to 60 seconds or until the mixture is smooth and the lovely pink color is visible.
3. The Rose Petal Radiance should be poured into a glass, garnished with a rose petal, and enjoyed.

PEPPERMINT ROSEMARY REVIVE

Preparation Time: 5 minutes

Cook Time: N/A

Serving: 1

Ingredients:

- 1 cup water
- 1 tablespoon fresh peppermint leaves
- 1 tablespoon fresh rosemary leaves
- 1/2 lemon, juiced
- 1 tablespoon honey
- 1/2 cup ice cubes

Instructions:

1. Combine the water, fresh rosemary and peppermint leaves, lemon juice, honey, and ice cubes in your Nutribullet blender.
2. Secure the lid on the blender, then blend the mixture on high for 45 to 60 seconds or until it is smooth and fragrant with rosemary and peppermint.
3. Enjoy this energizing and herbal-infused beverage by pouring the Peppermint Rosemary Revive into a glass and adding a sprig of fresh rosemary as a garnish.

ORANGE BLOSSOM BEAUTY

Preparation Time: 5 minutes

Cook Time: N/A

Serving: 1

Ingredients:

- 1 orange, peeled and segmented
- 1/2 cup carrots, chopped
- 1/2 cup plain Greek yogurt
- 1 tablespoon honey
- 1/2 teaspoon vanilla extract
- 1/2 cup ice cubes

Instructions:

1. Blend the ice cubes, Greek yogurt, honey, orange segments, diced carrots, and vanilla essence in the Nutribullet.
2. Secure the cover on the blender, then blend the mixture on high for 30 to 45 seconds or until it is smooth and creamy.
3. Pour the Orange Blossom Beauty into a glass, and then savor this energizing smoothie.

LEMON THYME TRANQUILITY

Preparation Time: 5 minutes

Cook Time: N/A

Serving: 1

Ingredients:

- 1 lemon, peeled and seeded
- 1 sprig of fresh thyme leaves
- 1/2 cup cucumber, diced
- 1/2 cup unsweetened coconut water
- 1 tablespoon honey
- 1/2 cup ice cubes

Instructions:

1. In the Nutribullet blender, combine the peeled and seeded lemon, fresh thyme leaves, chopped cucumber, coconut water, honey, and ice cubes.
2. Affix the cover to the blender and blend the mixture on high for 30 to 45 seconds or until it is smooth and reviving.
3. In a tumbler, pour the Lemon Thyme Tranquility, and savor this calming and energizing concoction.

HIBISCUS PASSION PUNCH

Preparation Time: 5 minutes

Cook Time: N/A

Serving: 1

Ingredients:

- 1/4 cup dried hibiscus petals (or 1 hibiscus tea bag)
- 1 cup boiling water
- 1/2 cup pineapple chunks
- 1/2 cup passion fruit pulp
- 1 tablespoon agave nectar
- 1/2 cup ice cubes

Instructions:

1. Hibiscus flowers (or a tea bag) should be steeped in boiling water for 5 minutes before letting it cool.
2. After cooling, combine the hibiscus tea, ice cubes, pineapple chunks, passion fruit pulp, agave nectar, and the Nutribullet.
3. Affix the cover to the blender and blend the mixture on high for 30 to 45 seconds or until it is creamy and bursting with tropical flavor.
4. Fill a glass with the Hibiscus Passion Punch and enjoy this unusual and cooling drink.

GINGER PEACH PERFECTION

Preparation Time: 5 minutes

Cook Time: N/A

Serving: 1

Ingredients:

- 1 ripe peach, pitted and sliced
- 1/2 inch fresh ginger
- 1/2 cup plain Greek yogurt
- 1 tablespoon honey
- 1/2 teaspoon ground cinnamon
- 1/2 cup ice cubes

Instructions:

1. Sliced ripe peaches, grated ginger, honey, cinnamon powder, Greek yogurt, and ice cubes should all be added to the Nutribullet mixer.
2. Secure the cover of the blender, then blend the mixture on high for 30 to 45 seconds or until it is creamy and overflowing with peachy sweetness.
3. Pour the Ginger Peach Perfection into a glass and enjoy the delicious harmony and advantageous health properties.

CINNAMON CLOVE COMFORT

Preparation Time: 5 minutes

Cook Time: N/A

Serving: 1

Ingredients:

- 1 banana, peeled and sliced
- 1/2 cup unsweetened almond milk
- 1/4 teaspoon ground cinnamon
- 1/8 teaspoon ground cloves
- 1 tablespoon honey
- 1/2 teaspoon vanilla extract
- 1/2 cup ice cubes

Instructions:

1. In the Nutribullet blender, combine the banana slices, almond milk, honey, vanilla essence, ground cinnamon, and ground cloves.
2. Affix the cover to the blender and blend the mixture on high for 30 to 45 seconds or until it is smooth and soothing.
3. Pour the Cinnamon Clove Comfort into a glass and savor the delicious smoothie's cozy and comforting taste.

SPEARMINT BERRY BREEZE

Preparation Time: 5 minutes

Cook Time: N/A

Serving: 1

Ingredients:

- 1/2 cup fresh spearmint leaves
- 1/2 cup mixed berries (strawberries, blueberries, raspberries)
- 1/2 cup unsweetened coconut water
- 1 tablespoon honey
- 1/2 teaspoon lime juice
- 1/2 cup ice cubes

Instructions:

1. In the Nutribullet blender, combine the fresh spearmint leaves, mixed berries, coconut water, honey, lime juice, and ice cubes.
2. The recommended blending time is 30 to 45 seconds on high or until the concoction is completely smooth and energetic.
3. The Spearmint Berry Breeze should be poured into a glass, and you should enjoy the cold, refreshing flavor of this minty berry treat.

CHAMOMILE LAVENDER LULLABY

Preparation Time: 5 minutes

Cook Time: N/A

Serving: 1

Ingredients:

- 1 chamomile tea bag
- 1 cup boiling water
- 1/2 cup ripe pear, diced
- 1/2 teaspoon dried lavender buds (food-grade)
- 1/2 cup plain Greek yogurt
- 1 tablespoon honey
- 1/2 cup ice cubes

Instructions:

1. The chamomile tea bag is at its most effective after being steeped in boiling water for 5 minutes.
2. The Nutribullet blender should be filled with ice cubes, Greek yogurt, honey, sliced pear, dried lavender buds, and chamomile tea once it has cooled.
3. Blend on high for generally 30 to 45 seconds or until the mixture is smooth and relaxing, with the lid firmly on the blender.
4. Get a glass of Chamomile Lavender Lullaby ready, then relax with this calming and fragrant smoothie.

VANILLA ROOIBOS EUPHORIA

Preparation Time: 5 minutes

Cook Time: N/A

Serving: 1

Ingredients:

- 1 vanilla rooibos tea bag
- 1 cup boiling water
- 1/2 cup mango chunks
- 1/2 cup pineapple chunks
- 1/2 cup plain Greek yogurt
- 1 tablespoon honey
- 1/2 cup ice cubes

Instructions:

1. Allow the vanilla rooibos tea bag to cool after 5 minutes of steeping in hot water.
2. Once chilled, put the ice cubes, Greek yogurt, honey, mango, pineapple, and vanilla rooibos tea in the Nutribullet mixer.
3. When the liquid is smooth and deliciously flavored, often after around 30-45 seconds on high, lock the blender cover and continue blending.
4. In a glass, pour the Vanilla Rooibos Euphoria, and savor this unusual and wonderful smoothie.

LEMON BALM BERRY BOOST

Preparation Time: 5 minutes

Cook Time: N/A

Serving: 1

Ingredients:

- 1 cup mixed berries (strawberries, blueberries, raspberries)
- 1/2 cup Greek yogurt
- 1 tablespoon honey
- 1/2 lemon, juiced
- 1 sprig of fresh lemon balm leaves
- 1/2 cup water
- 1 cup ice cubes

Instructions:

1. In your Nutribullet blender, combine mixed berries, Greek yogurt, honey, lemon juice, lemon balm leaves, water, and ice cubes.
2. Secure the cover on the blender, then blend the mixture on high for 30 to 45 seconds or until it is smooth and creamy.
3. Enjoy the blast of berry flavor with the Lemon Balm Berry Boost in a glass!

LAVENDER PEACH SERENADE

Preparation Time: 5 minutes

Cook Time: N/A

Serving: 1

Ingredients:

- 1 ripe peach, pitted and sliced
- 1/2 cup plain yogurt
- 1 tablespoon honey
- 1/2 teaspoon dried culinary lavender buds
- 1/2 cup almond milk
- 1 cup ice cubes

Instructions:

1. In your Nutribullet blender, combine the following Ingredients: peach slices, plain yogurt, honey, dried lavender buds, almond milk, and ice cubes.
2. Don't remove the blender's cover until the liquid is completely smooth and aromatic with lavender after blending on high for 30-45 seconds.
3. Enjoy the calming and aromatic Lavender Peach Serenade by pouring it into a glass.

CRANBERRY ORANGE SPICE

Preparation Time: 5 minutes

Cook Time: N/A

Serving: 1

Ingredients:

- 1/2 cup cranberries (fresh or frozen)
- 1 orange, peeled and segmented
- 1/2 teaspoon ground cinnamon
- 1/4 teaspoon ground nutmeg
- 1 tablespoon honey
- 1/2 cup orange juice
- 1 cup ice cubes

Instructions:

1. In your Nutribullet blender, combine the cranberries, orange segments, honey, cinnamon, nutmeg, and ice cubes.
2. When the mixture is smooth and has a nice balance of tartness and spice, blend on high for about 30-45 seconds with the lid securely on the blender.
3. In a glass, pour the Cranberry Orange Spice, and savor this tangy and fragrant concoction.

TURMERIC CARDAMOM BLISS

Preparation Time: 5 minutes

Cook Time: N/A

Serving: 1

Ingredients:

- 1 banana, peeled
- 1/2 teaspoon ground turmeric
- 1/4 teaspoon ground cardamom

- 1 tablespoon honey
- 1 cup unsweetened coconut milk
- 1 cup ice cubes

Instructions:

1. Put the banana, honey, coconut milk, ground turmeric, ground cardamom, and ice cubes in your Nutribullet mixer.
2. When the mixture is smooth, creamy, and flavorful of heat and spice, secure the cover of the blender and blend on high for generally 30 to 45 seconds.
3. In a glass, pour the Turmeric Cardamom Bliss, and savor this unusual and nutritious concoction.

GREEN TEA MANGO TANGO

Preparation Time: 5 minutes

Cook Time: N/A

Serving: 1

Ingredients:

- 1 green tea bag, brewed and cooled
- 1 cup frozen mango chunks
- 1/2 cup spinach leaves
- 1 tablespoon honey
- 1/2 cup almond milk
- 1 cup ice cubes

Instructions:

1. Prepare some green tea, and after it has cooled, discard the tea bag.
2. In your Nutribullet blender, combine the brewed green tea, frozen mango chunks, spinach leaves, honey, almond milk, and ice cubes.
3. Affix the cover to the blender and run it on high for 30 to 45 seconds or until the mixture is smooth and a bright green color.
4. Enjoy the reviving and antioxidant-rich flavor of the Green Tea Mango Tango by pouring it into a glass.

STRAWBERRY BASIL DETOX

Preparation Time: 5 minutes

Cook Time: N/A

Serving: 1

Ingredients:

- 1 cup fresh strawberries, hulled
- 1/4 cup fresh basil leaves
- 1 tablespoon honey
- 1/2 lemon, juiced
- 1/2 cucumber, peeled and sliced
- 1/2 cup water
- 1 cup ice cubes

Instructions:

1. In your Nutribullet blender, combine fresh strawberries, basil leaves, honey, lemon juice, cucumber slices, water, and ice cubes.
2. Affix the cover to the blender and run it on high for 30 to 45 seconds or until the mixture is smooth and tastes herbaceous and refreshing.
3. The Strawberry Basil Detox should be poured into a glass, and you may enjoy the refreshing and purifying qualities of this delicious smoothie.

BERRY BLAST SMOOTHIE

Preparation Time: 5 minutes

Cook Time: 0 minutes

Serving: 2

Ingredients:

- 1 cup mixed berries (strawberries, blueberries, raspberries)
- 1 ripe banana
- 1/2 cup Greek yogurt
- 1/2 cup almond milk
- 1 tablespoon honey
- 1 cup ice cubes

Instructions:

1. Your Nutribullet blender should now include Greek yogurt, ripe banana, mixed berries, almond milk, honey, and ice cubes.
2. After closing the lid, combine the ingredients for at least 30 seconds or until they reach a creamy consistency.
3. Pour the Berry Blast Smoothie into glasses, and savor it!

BANANA SPLIT DELIGHT

Preparation Time: 5 minutes

Cook Time: 0 minutes

Serving: 2

Ingredients:

- 2 ripe bananas
- 1/2 cup pineapple chunks
- 1/4 cup unsweetened cocoa powder
- 1 cup almond milk
- 1/4 cup chopped walnuts
- 1 tablespoon honey
- 1 cup ice cubes

Instructions:

1. In your Nutribullet blender, combine the ripe bananas, pineapple pieces, cocoa powder, almond milk, walnuts that have been diced, honey, and ice cubes.
2. Blend for about 45 seconds, or until the smoothie is smooth and creamy, with the lid tightly on the blender.
3. Enjoy the taste of a Banana Split Delight after pouring into glasses!

GREEN APPLE CRUNCH

Preparation Time: 5 minutes

Cook Time: 0 minutes

Serving: 2

Ingredients:

- 2 green apples, cored and sliced
- 1 cup spinach leaves
- 1/2 cucumber, peeled and chopped
- 1/2 lemon, juiced
- 1 tablespoon honey
- 1 cup water
- 1 cup ice cubes

Instructions:

1. In your Nutribullet blender, combine the green apples, spinach leaves, cucumber, lemon juice, honey, water, and ice cubes.
2. For a smooth and energizing Green Apple Crunch smoothie, mix for around 45 seconds with the lid on the blender.
3. Pour this wholesome, green treat into glasses and savor it!

TROPICAL PARADISE SHAKE

Preparation Time: 5 minutes

Cook Time: 0 minutes

Serving: 2

Ingredients:

- 1 cup frozen pineapple chunks
- 1/2 cup frozen mango chunks
- 1/2 banana
- 1/2 cup coconut milk
- 1/2 cup Greek yogurt
- 1 tablespoon honey
- 1/2 cup ice cubes

Instructions:

1. In your Nutribullet blender, combine the frozen pineapple chunks, frozen mango chunks, banana, coconut milk, Greek yogurt, honey, and ice cubes.
2. It normally takes 45 seconds to combine the ingredients until it is creamy and tastes like a tropical paradise with the lid securely on.
3. Pour into glasses, then take a taste of heaven.

RAINBOW VEGGIE SURPRISE

Preparation Time: 10 minutes

Cook Time: 0 minutes

Serving: 2

Ingredients:

- 1/2 cup baby carrots
- 1/2 cup cherry tomatoes
- 1/2 cup red bell pepper, chopped
- 1/2 cucumber, chopped
- 1/2 cup spinach leaves
- 1/2 cup water
- 1/2 lemon, juiced
- Salt and pepper to taste
- 1 cup ice cubes

Instructions:

1. To your Nutribullet blender, add the baby carrots, cherry tomatoes, red bell pepper, cucumber, spinach leaves, water, lemon juice, salt, and ice cubes.
2. Blend for around 45 seconds, with the cover on tightly, to create a colorful Rainbow Veggie Surprise smoothie.
3. Pour into glasses, add a cherry tomato or cucumber slice as a garnish, and savor this wholesome and eye-catching drink!

CREAMY ALMOND BERRY DREAM

Preparation Time: 5 minutes

Cook Time: 0 minutes

Serving: 2

Ingredients:

- 1/2 cup mixed berries (strawberries, blueberries, raspberries)
- 1/2 cup almond butter

- 1 cup almond milk
- 1 tablespoon honey
- 1/2 teaspoon vanilla extract
- 1 cup ice cubes

Instructions:

1. In your Nutribullet blender, combine the mixed berries, almond butter, almond milk, honey, vanilla extract, and ice cubes.
2. Blend the ingredients for about 30 seconds, with the lid on the blender, or until the mixture is creamy and you have a Creamy Almond Berry Dream.
3. Enjoy the creamy, nutty, and berry sweetness after pouring it into glasses!

PEACHY KEEN POWER PUNCH

Preparation Time: 5 minutes

Cook Time: 0 minutes

Serving: 2

Ingredients:

- 2 ripe peaches, pitted and sliced
- 1/2 cup plain Greek yogurt
- 1/2 cup orange juice
- 1 tablespoon honey
- 1/2 teaspoon grated ginger
- 1 cup ice cubes

Instructions:

1. In your Nutribullet blender, combine the ripe peaches, Greek yogurt, orange juice, honey, chopped ginger, and ice cubes.
2. It usually takes 30 seconds or less to combine the ingredients until the liquid is smooth and you have a Peachy Keen Power Punch.
3. Pour the delicious peachy sweetness into glasses and savor it!

SPINACH SUPERHERO SMOOTHIE

Preparation Time: 5 minutes

Cook Time: N/A

Serving: 1

Ingredients:

- 1 cup fresh spinach leaves
- 1 banana, peeled
- 1/2 cup pineapple chunks (fresh or frozen)
- 1/2 cup Greek yogurt
- 1 tablespoon honey
- 1/2 cup water
- 1 cup ice cubes

Instructions:

1. In your Nutribullet blender, combine the fresh spinach leaves, banana, pineapple pieces, Greek yogurt, honey, water, and ice cubes.
2. Affix the cover to the blender and run it on high for 45 to 60 seconds or until the mixture is smooth and bright green.
3. Fill a glass with the spinach superhero smoothie and savor this nutrient-rich, potent beverage!

BLUEBERRY BLAST-OFF

Preparation Time: 5 minutes

Cook Time: N/A

Serving: 1

Ingredients:

- 1/2 cup blueberries (fresh or frozen)
- 1/2 cup Greek yogurt
- 1/2 cup almond milk
- 1 tablespoon honey
- 1/4 teaspoon vanilla extract
- 1/2 cup ice cubes

Instructions:

1. In your Nutribullet blender, combine the blueberries, Greek yogurt, almond milk, honey, vanilla extract, and ice cubes.
2. Keep the blender's cover on and blend for 30 to 45 seconds on high or until the mixture is silky smooth and bursting with blueberry flavor.
3. Pour the Blueberry Blast-Off into a glass, then savor this wonderful smoothie that is packed with antioxidants.

ORANGE CREAMSICLE CRUSH

Preparation Time: 5 minutes

Cook Time: N/A

Serving: 1

Ingredients:

- 1 orange, peeled and segmented
- 1/2 cup Greek yogurt
- 1/2 cup almond milk
- 1 tablespoon honey
- 1/4 teaspoon vanilla extract
- 1/2 cup ice cubes

Instructions:

1. In your Nutribullet blender, combine the orange segments, Greek yogurt, almond milk, honey, vanilla essence, and ice cubes.
2. Closing the blender's lid and processing it on high for 30 to 45 seconds usually results in a smooth concoction with the classic creamsicle taste.
3. Fill a glass with Orange Creamsicle Crush and enjoy the delicious treat's nostalgic flavor!

CARROT CAKE SMOOTHIE

Preparation Time: 5 minutes

Cook Time: N/A

Serving: 1

Ingredients:

- 1 medium carrot, peeled and chopped
- 1/2 cup rolled oats
- 1/2 cup Greek yogurt
- 1 tablespoon honey
- 1/4 teaspoon ground cinnamon
- 1/4 teaspoon ground nutmeg
- 1/2 cup almond milk
- 1/2 cup ice cubes

Instructions:

1. Put the Greek yogurt, honey, cinnamon, nutmeg, ground carrot, rolled oats, almond milk, and ice cubes into your Nutribullet blender.
2. It should take between 45 and 60 seconds to smooth out the mixture and give it a carrot cake-like flavor while blending on high.
3. Fill a glass with the carrot cake smoothie and savor the taste of a beloved dessert in a healthy smoothie!

STRAWBERRY BANANA BONANZA

Preparation Time: 5 minutes

Cook Time: N/A

Serving: 1

Ingredients:

- 1/2 cup strawberries (fresh or frozen)
- 1 banana, peeled
- 1/2 cup Greek yogurt
- 1 tablespoon honey
- 1/2 cup almond milk
- 1/2 cup ice cubes

Instructions:

1. In your Nutribullet blender, combine the strawberries, banana, Greek yogurt, honey, almond milk, and ice cubes.
2. Make sure the blender top is on and mix for 30–45 seconds on high or until the drink is completely smooth and bursting with flavor.
3. In a glass, pour the Strawberry Banana Bonanza, and savor this time-honored taste combination!

KIWI BERRY BURST

Preparation Time: 5 minutes

Cook Time: N/A

Serving: 1

Ingredients:

- 2 kiwis, peeled and chopped
- 1/2 cup mixed berries (strawberries, blueberries, raspberries - fresh or frozen)
- 1/2 cup Greek yogurt
- 1 tablespoon honey
- 1/2 cup water
- 1 cup ice cubes

Instructions:

1. In your Nutribullet blender, combine the diced kiwis, mixed berries, Greek yogurt, honey, water, and ice cubes.
2. Cover the blender and blend for 45-60 seconds on high until the mixture is completely smooth and vibrant in color.
3. Pour the Kiwi Berry Burst into a glass, then savor this smoothie that is full of antioxidants and is refreshing.

CUCUMBER COOL-DOWN

Preparation Time: 5 minutes

Cook Time: N/A

Serving: 1

Ingredients:

- 1 cucumber, peeled and chopped
- 1/2 cup plain Greek yogurt
- 1/2 cup fresh mint leaves
- 1 tablespoon honey
- 1/2 cup ice cubes

Instructions:

1. Blender the cucumber, ice cubes, Greek yogurt, honey, fresh mint leaves, and mint oil.
2. Secure the cover on the blender, then blend on high for, typically, 30-45 seconds or until the mixture is smooth and creamy.
3. The Cucumber Cool-Down should be poured into a glass, garnished with a mint sprig, and then enjoyed.

PINEAPPLE PASSION POTION

Preparation Time: 5 minutes

Cook Time: N/A

Serving: 1

Ingredients:

- 1 cup fresh pineapple chunks
- 1/2 cup coconut milk
- 1/2 banana, peeled
- 1 tablespoon honey
- 1/2 teaspoon vanilla extract
- 1/2 cup ice cubes

Instructions:

1. Blend together in the Nutribullet the fresh pineapple chunks, coconut milk, banana, honey, vanilla essence, and ice cubes.
2. Affix the cover to the blender and blend the mixture on high for 45 to 60 seconds or until it is smooth and tropical-flavored.
3. Fill a glass with the Pineapple Passion Potion and savor the taste of the tropics.

PEANUT BUTTER & JELLY JOLT

Preparation Time: 5 minutes

Cook Time: N/A

Serving: 1

Ingredients:

- 2 tablespoons natural peanut butter
- 1/2 cup mixed berries (strawberries, raspberries, blueberries)

- 1/2 banana, peeled
- 1 cup unsweetened almond milk
- 1 tablespoon honey
- 1/2 cup ice cubes

Instructions:

1. In the Nutribullet blender, combine natural peanut butter, mixed berries, bananas, almond milk, honey, and ice cubes.
2. Lock the lid of the blender and blend the mixture on high for 45 to 60 seconds or until it is smooth and resembles a traditional PB&J sandwich.
3. Enjoy this flavor by pouring the Peanut Butter and jelly Jolt into a glass.

WATERMELON WONDER

Preparation Time: 5 minutes

Cook Time: N/A

Serving: 1

Ingredients:

- 2 cups fresh watermelon chunks, seeds removed
- 1/2 lime, juiced
- 1 tablespoon honey
- 1/2 cup ice cubes

Instructions:

1. The Nutribullet blender should be filled with fresh watermelon pieces, lime juice, honey, and ice cubes.
2. When the liquid is smooth and very refreshing, often after around 30-45 seconds on high, lock the blender cover and continue blending.
3. In a glass, pour the Watermelon Wonder, top with a lime slice, and savor the taste of summer.

CHERRY CHOCOLATE CHIP SHAKE

Preparation Time: 5 minutes

Cook Time: N/A

Serving: 1

Ingredients:

- 1/2 cup frozen cherries
- 1 tablespoon cocoa powder
- 1 tablespoon chocolate chips
- 1/2 cup Greek yogurt
- 1/2 cup almond milk
- 1 tablespoon honey
- 1/2 cup ice cubes

Instructions:

1. In the Nutribullet blender, combine frozen cherries, cocoa powder, chocolate chips, Greek yogurt, almond milk, honey, and ice cubes.
2. Affix the cover to the blender and blend the mixture on high for 45 to 60 seconds or until it is smooth and chocolaty.
3. Fill a glass with the Cherry Chocolate Chip Shake and enjoy this dessert-like delight.

SWEET POTATO PIE SMOOTHIE

Preparation Time: 8 minutes (includes roasting sweet potato)

Cook Time: N/A

Serving: 1

Ingredients:

- 1 small sweet potato, roasted and peeled
- 1/2 banana, peeled
- 1/2 teaspoon ground cinnamon
- 1/4 teaspoon ground nutmeg
- 1/2 cup plain Greek yogurt
- 1 tablespoon honey
- 1/2 cup almond milk
- 1/2 cup ice cubes

Instructions:

1. In a 375°F/190°C oven, roast the sweet potato for about 45 minutes or until it is fork-tender. Peel and cut it after allowing it to cool.
2. Blend the roasted sweet potato, banana, Greek yogurt, honey, almond milk, cinnamon, nutmeg, and ice cubes in the Nutribullet.
3. Fasten the blender's cover and blend the ingredients for 45 to 60 seconds or until they are smooth and reminiscent of sweet potato pie.
4. Take a sip of the seasonal tastes after pouring the sweet potato pie smoothie into a glass and topping it with a touch of cinnamon.

RASPBERRY LEMONADE SPLASH

Preparation Time: 5 minutes

Cook Time: N/A

Serving: 1

Ingredients:

- 1 cup fresh raspberries
- 1/2 lemon, juiced
- 1 tablespoon honey
- 1 cup water
- 1/2 cup ice cubes

Instructions:

1. Blend the Nutribullet with fresh raspberries, lemon juice, honey, water, and ice cubes.
2. Affix the cover to the blender and blend the ingredients on high for 30 to 45 seconds or until it is smooth and tartly refreshing.
3. In a glass, pour the Raspberry Lemonade Splash, top with a lemon slice, and savor this citrusy treat.

AVOCADO AVENGER BLEND

Preparation Time: 5 minutes

Cook Time: N/A

Serving: 1

Ingredients:

- 1 ripe avocado, peeled and pitted
- 1/2 cup spinach leaves
- 1/2 cucumber, peeled and chopped
- 1/2 lemon, juiced
- 1/2 cup coconut water
- 1/2 cup ice cubes

Instructions:

1. Put spinach leaves, diced cucumber, ripe avocados, coconut water, lemon juice, and ice cubes in the Nutribullet mixer.
2. Secure the cover of the blender, then blend the mixture on high for 45 to 60 seconds or until it is smooth and full of wholesome greens.
3. The Avocado Avenger Blend should be poured into a glass, topped with a slice of cucumber, and enjoyed.

CARROT ORANGE ZEST

Preparation Time: 5 minutes

Cook Time: N/A

Serving: 1

Ingredients:

- 2 medium carrots, peeled and chopped
- 1 orange, peeled and segmented
- 1/2 lemon, juiced

- 1 tablespoon honey
- 1/2 cup water
- 1/2 cup ice cubes

Instructions:

1. In the Nutribullet blender, combine the diced carrots, orange segments, honey, lemon juice, water, and ice cubes.
2. Put the top on the blender, and blend the ingredients for 45 to 60 seconds or until the mixture is completely smooth and tastes like an explosion of citrus.
3. Enjoy this vitamin-rich treat by adding the Carrot Orange Zest to a glass, garnishing with an orange twist.

APPLE CINNAMON CRUNCH

Preparation Time: 5 minutes

Cook Time: N/A

Serving: 1

Ingredients:

- 1 apple, cored and chopped
- 1/2 teaspoon ground cinnamon
- 1/4 teaspoon ground nutmeg
- 1/2 cup rolled oats
- 1 tablespoon honey
- 1 cup almond milk
- 1/2 cup ice cubes

Instructions:

1. In the Nutribullet blender, combine the diced apple, ground cinnamon, ground nutmeg, rolled oats, honey, almond milk, and ice cubes.
2. When the mixture is smooth and resembles a warm apple pie, secure the cover of the blender and process on high for typically 45 to 60 seconds.
3. Pour some Apple Cinnamon Crunch into a glass, top with more cinnamon, and savor the flavor of a hearty breakfast.

BANANA BLUEBERRY BOOSTER

Preparation Time: 5 minutes

Cook Time: N/A

Serving: 1

Ingredients:

- 1 ripe banana
- 1/2 cup blueberries (fresh or frozen)
- 1/2 cup Greek yogurt
- 1 tablespoon honey
- 1/2 cup almond milk
- 1/2 teaspoon vanilla extract
- 1 cup ice cubes

Instructions:

1. In your Nutribullet blender, combine the banana, blueberries, Greek yogurt, honey, almond milk, vanilla extract, and ice cubes.
2. With the lid securely on, blend the ingredients for at least 45 seconds or until you get a smooth consistency.
3. The Banana Blueberry Booster should be poured into a glass for your nutrient-rich smoothie.

PEANUT BUTTER CUP PARADISE

Preparation Time: 5 minutes

Cook Time: N/A

Serving: 1

Ingredients:

- 1 banana, peeled
- 2 tablespoons natural peanut butter
- 1 tablespoon cocoa powder
- 1 tablespoon honey
- 1 cup almond milk
- 1/2 teaspoon vanilla extract
- 1 cup ice cubes

Instructions:

1. In your Nutribullet blender, combine the banana, peanut butter, chocolate powder, honey, almond milk, vanilla extract, and ice cubes.
2. Blend the ingredients for generally 30 to 45 seconds or until it is smooth and creamy. Secure the blender top.
3. Pour the Peanut Butter Cup Paradise into a glass and enjoy your smoothie while enjoying the delicious fusion of peanut butter and chocolate tastes!

VEGGIE RAINBOW RIOT

Preparation Time: 7 minutes

Cook Time: N/A

Serving: 1

Ingredients:

- 1/2 cup baby spinach
- 1/2 small carrot, peeled and chopped
- 1/4 small beetroot, peeled and chopped
- 1/4 red bell pepper, chopped
- 1/4 small cucumber, chopped
- 1/2 tomato, chopped
- 1/4 small red onion, chopped
- 1/2 cup water
- 1 tablespoon lemon juice
- Salt and pepper to taste
- Ice cubes (optional)

Instructions:

1. In your Nutribullet blender, combine the spinach, carrot, beetroot, red bell pepper, cucumber, tomato, and red onion.
2. Blender Ingredients: water, lemon juice, and ice cubes (if using).
3. Blend for generally 1-2 minutes, until the mixture is smooth and all the components are thoroughly incorporated. Secure the blender cap.
4. To taste, season the food with salt and pepper.
5. Pour a glass of the Veggie Rainbow Riot, then savor this colorful and nutrient-rich veggie smoothie!

COCONUT MANGO MADNESS

Preparation Time: 5 minutes

Cook Time: N/A

Serving: 1

Ingredients:

- 1 cup fresh mango chunks (about 1 medium-sized mango)
- 1/2 cup coconut milk
- 1/2 cup Greek yogurt
- 1 tablespoon honey (adjust to taste)
- 1/4 cup shredded coconut
- 1/2 teaspoon vanilla extract
- 1 cup ice cubes

Instructions:

1. Prep the Mango: Peel and chop the fresh mango into chunks. Make sure to remove the pit.
2. Blend: Place the mango chunks, coconut milk, Greek yogurt, honey, shredded coconut, vanilla extract, and ice cubes into your Nutribullet blender.
3. Blend Until Smooth: Secure the blender lid and blend on high until the mixture is smooth and creamy. This usually takes about 45-60 seconds, depending on the power of your blender.
4. Adjust the sweetness by adding additional honey, if required, after tasting the Coconut Mango Madness. Blend again briefly to incorporate any additional honey.
5. Serve: Pour the creamy Coconut Mango Madness into a glass. For an extra island flair, you may top it up with some shredded coconut or a mango slice.
6. Enjoy: Savor the smooth blend of tropical mango and coconut milk. It's a delicious and healthful snack or light breakfast option that's quick to prepare.

GREEN GRAPES GALORE

Preparation Time: 5 minutes

Cook Time: N/A

Serving: 1

Ingredients:

- 1 cup green grapes
- 1/2 cup spinach leaves
- 1/2 cup cucumber slices
- 1/4 cup plain yogurt
- 1 tablespoon honey
- 1/2 cup ice cubes

Instructions:

1. The Nutribullet blender should be filled with green grapes, spinach leaves, cucumber slices, plain yogurt, honey, and ice cubes.
2. Secure the cover on the blender and run it on high for 45 to 60 seconds or until the mixture is smooth and the bright green color is visible.
3. Enjoy the hydrating and nutritious green deliciousness after pouring some Green Grapes Galore into a glass.

VANILLA ALMOND BERRY BLISS

Preparation Time: 5 minutes

Cook Time: N/A

Serving: 1

Ingredients:

- 1/2 cup mixed berries (strawberries, blueberries, raspberries)
- 1/2 cup almond milk
- 1/4 cup Greek yogurt
- 1 tablespoon honey
- 1/2 teaspoon vanilla extract
- 1/2 cup ice cubes

Instructions:

1. In the Nutribullet blender, combine the mixed berries, almond milk, Greek yogurt, honey, vanilla extract, and ice cubes.
2. Lock the lid of the blender and blend the mixture on high for 45 to 60 seconds or until it is smooth and overflowing with berry sweetness.
3. Fill a glass with the Vanilla Almond Berry Bliss and savor the delicious flavor combination!

BLACKBERRY BLAST-OFF

Preparation Time: 5 minutes

Cook Time: 0 minutes

Serving: 1

Ingredients:

- 1 cup fresh blackberries
- 1/2 cup plain Greek yogurt
- 1/2 cup unsweetened almond milk
- 1 tablespoon honey
- 1/2 teaspoon vanilla extract
- 1 cup ice cubes

Instructions:

1. In the Nutribullet blender, combine the fresh blackberries, Greek yogurt, almond milk, honey, vanilla essence, and ice cubes.
2. Lock the lid of the blender and run it on high for 45 to 60 seconds or until the liquid is smooth and the blackberries are well combined.
3. Pour the Blackberry Blast-Off into a glass, then sip on this smoothie filled with antioxidants while it's still cold.

SWEET SPINACH SURPRISE

Preparation Time: 5 minutes

Cook Time: 0 minutes

Serving: 1

Ingredients:

- 1 cup fresh spinach leaves
- 1/2 banana, peeled
- 1/2 cup pineapple chunks (fresh or frozen)
- 1/2 cup unsweetened coconut water
- 1 tablespoon chia seeds (optional)
- 1 cup ice cubes

Instructions:

1. Put the banana, pineapple chunks, coconut water, chia seeds (if using), and ice cubes in the Nutribullet mixer along with the fresh spinach leaves.
2. Secure the cover on the blender and run it on high for 45 to 60 seconds or until the mixture is smooth and the bright green color is visible.
3. Enjoy this wholesome and delectable green smoothie by pouring the Sweet Spinach Surprise into a glass.

CHOCOLATE COVERED CHERRY DELIGHT

Preparation Time: 5 minutes

Cook Time: 0 minutes

Serving: 1

Ingredients:

- 1/2 cup frozen cherries
- 1 tablespoon unsweetened cocoa powder
- 1/2 cup unsweetened almond milk
- 1 tablespoon honey or maple syrup
- 1/2 teaspoon vanilla extract
- 1 cup ice cubes

Instructions:

1. In the Nutribullet blender, combine the frozen cherries, cocoa powder, almond milk, honey or maple syrup, vanilla extract, and ice cubes.
2. Secure the lid on the blender and run it on high for 45 to 60 seconds or until the mixture is rich, creamy, and chocolaty.
3. Take a sip of your Chocolate Covered Cherry Delight and enjoy this tasty, nutritious treat with chocolate taste!

BEETROOT BERRY BURST

Preparation Time: 5 minutes

Cook Time: 0 minutes

Serving: 1

Ingredients:

- 1 small beetroot, peeled and chopped
- 1/2 cup mixed berries (strawberries, blueberries, raspberries)
- 1/2 cup plain Greek yogurt
- 1 tablespoon honey
- 1/2 cup water
- 1 cup ice cubes

Instructions:

1. The Nutribullet blender should be filled with diced beets, mixed berries, Greek yogurt, honey, water, and ice cubes.
2. Fasten the blender's cover and blend the ingredients on high for 45 to 60 seconds or until silky smooth and a vibrant pink color is achieved.
3. Place the Beetroot Berry Burst in a glass and savor this colorful, antioxidant-rich smoothie!

HONEYDEW MELON MAGIC

Preparation Time: 5 minutes

Cook Time: 0 minutes

Serving: 1

Ingredients:

- 1 cup diced honeydew melon
- 1/2 cup cucumber, peeled and chopped
- 1/2 lime, juiced
- 1 tablespoon honey
- 1/2 cup coconut water
- 1 cup ice cubes

Instructions:

1. Honeydew melon sliced, cucumber cut, lime juice, honey, coconut water, and ice cubes should all be added to the Nutribullet mixer.
2. Secure the cover on the blender and run it on high for 45 to 60 seconds or until the mixture is smooth and the vibrant green color comes through
3. Enjoy this refreshing and delicious smoothie made with melon by pouring the Honeydew Melon Magic into a glass.

GREEN GODDESS DETOX SMOOTHIE

Preparation Time: 5 minutes

Cook Time: N/A

Serving: 1

Ingredients:

- 1 cup kale, stems removed
- 1/2 cucumber, peeled and chopped
- 1/2 green apple, cored and sliced
- 1/2 lemon, juiced
- 1 tablespoon fresh ginger, peeled and minced
- 1 cup coconut water
- 1 cup ice cubes

Instructions:

1. Combine the kale, cucumber, green apple, lemon juice, ginger, and coconut water in the Nutrillet blender.
2. Add the ice cubes on top of the remaining ingredients.
3. Attach the lid to the blender, and then blend the mixture for 45 to 60 seconds on high or until it is smooth and a vibrant green color.
4. Start your day off well by filling a glass with the Green Goddess Detox Smoothie!

BERRY BLAST METABOLISM BOOSTER

Preparation Time: 5 minutes

Cook Time: N/A

Serving: 1

Ingredients:

- 1 cup mixed berries (strawberries, blueberries, raspberries)
- 1/2 cup Greek yogurt
- 1 tablespoon honey
- 1/4 teaspoon cayenne pepper (adjust to taste)
- 1 cup almond milk
- 1 cup ice cubes

Instructions:

1. In a Nutribullet, combine Greek yogurt, honey, cayenne, and mixed berries.
2. You should include almond milk and ice cubes.
3. Lock the lid of the blender when the mixture is smooth and has a burst of berry taste, usually after 30-45 seconds of mixing on high.
4. Add some Berry Blast Metabolism Booster to a glass to speed up your metabolism.

TROPICAL PARADISE PROTEIN SHAKE

Preparation Time: 5 minutes

Cook Time: N/A

Serving: 1

Ingredients:

- 1/2 cup pineapple chunks
- 1/2 banana
- 1/2 cup coconut milk
- 1/2 cup Greek yogurt
- 1 scoop vanilla protein powder
- 1 tablespoon honey
- 1 cup ice cubes

Instructions:

1. The pineapple chunks, banana, coconut milk, Greek yogurt, vanilla protein powder, and honey should all be combined in a NutriBullet.
2. Add the ice cubes on top of the remaining ingredients.
3. Attach the cover to the blender, then mix the ingredients for 45 to 60 seconds on high or until they are smooth and flavorful of the tropics.
4. Pouring the Tropical Paradise Protein Shake into a glass will make you feel as though you're in a tropical paradise.

SPINACH AND PINEAPPLE SLIMDOWN

Preparation Time: 5 minutes

Cook Time: N/A

Serving: 1

Ingredients:

- 1 cup fresh spinach leaves
- 1/2 cup pineapple chunks
- 1/2 lime, juiced
- 1/4 avocado

- 1 tablespoon chia seeds
- 1 cup coconut water
- 1 cup ice cubes

Instructions:

1. In the NutriBullet blender, combine the chia seeds, avocado, pineapple chunks, lime juice, and fresh spinach leaves.
2. Coconut water and ice cubes should be included.
3. Blend the mixture on high for 45 to 60 seconds or until it is smooth and green while securing the cover of the blender.
4. To reduce weight in a healthy way, pour yourself a glass of Spinach and Pineapple Slimdown!

BLUEBERRY ALMOND BLISS

Preparation Time: 5 minutes

Cook Time: N/A

Serving: 1

Ingredients:

- 1/2 cup blueberries
- 1/4 cup almonds
- 1/2 cup Greek yogurt
- 1 tablespoon honey
- 1/2 teaspoon vanilla extract
- 1 cup almond milk
- 1 cup ice cubes

Instructions:

1. Blueberries, almonds, Greek yogurt, honey, and vanilla extract are combined in a NutriBullet.
2. Add almond milk and ice cubes.
3. Close the blender's lid and blend the ingredients for 30 to 45 seconds on high speed or until the smoothie is perfectly smooth and bursting with blueberry flavor.
4. Pour the Blueberry Almond Bliss into a glass and savor the flavor!

CHOCOLATE PEANUT BUTTER POWERHOUSE

Preparation Time: 5 minutes

Cook Time: N/A

Serving: 1

Ingredients:

- 1 banana, peeled
- 2 tablespoons natural peanut butter
- 1 tablespoon cocoa powder
- 1 tablespoon honey
- 1 cup unsweetened almond milk
- 1 cup ice cubes

Instructions:

1. Bananas, natural peanut butter, chocolate powder, honey, and almond milk should all be blended in a NutriBullet.
2. Add the ice cubes on top of the remaining ingredients.
3. Keep the cover on the blender and process for 30–45 seconds until the mixture is silky smooth and chocolatey.
4. Take a sip of the delectable yet healthy Chocolate Peanut Butter Powerhouse to increase your energy.

KALE AND MANGO MAGIC

Preparation Time: 5 minutes

Cook Time: N/A

Serving: 1

Ingredients:

- 1 cup kale, stems removed
- 1/2 cup mango chunks
- 1/2 banana
- 1/2 lime, juiced
- 1 tablespoon honey
- 1 cup coconut water
- 1 cup ice cubes

Instructions:

1. Combine the kale, mango chunks, banana, lime juice, and honey in the Nutribullet mixer.
2. Coconut water and ice cubes should be included.
3. When the mixture is smooth and packed with the amazing flavor of kale and mango, lock the lid of the blender and blend it on high for 45 to 60 seconds.
4. Enjoy the enjoyment by adding some Kale and Mango Magic to a tumbler.

CUCUMBER MINT COOLER

Preparation Time: 5 minutes

Cook Time: N/A

Serving: 1

Ingredients:

- 1 cucumber, peeled and chopped
- 1/2 cup fresh mint leaves
- 1/2 lemon, juiced
- 1 tablespoon honey
- 1 cup water
- 1 cup ice cubes

Instructions:

1. Blend the cucumber, fresh mint leaves, lemon juice, and honey in the NutriBullet.
2. Add water and ice cubes.
3. Lock the blender cover and continue mixing till the liquid is silky and delightfully cooling, usually after around 30-45 seconds on high.
4. Pouring the Cucumber Mint Cooler into a glass is required. Enjoy this refreshing beverage to unwind.

GREEN GODDESS DETOX SMOOTHIE

Preparation Time: 5 minutes

Cook Time: N/A

Serving: 1

Ingredients:

- 1 cup kale, stems removed
- 1/2 cucumber, peeled and chopped
- 1/2 green apple, cored and sliced
- 1/2 lemon, juiced
- 1 tablespoon fresh ginger, peeled and minced
- 1 cup coconut water
- 1 cup ice cubes

Instructions:

1. Combine the kale, cucumber, green apple, lemon juice, ginger, and coconut water in the Nutrillet blender.
2. Add the ice cubes on top of the remaining ingredients.
3. Attach the lid to the blender, and then blend the mixture for 45 to 60 seconds on high or until it is smooth and a vibrant green color.
4. Start your day off well by filling a glass with the Green Goddess Detox Smoothie!

BERRY BLAST METABOLISM BOOSTER

Preparation Time: 5 minutes

Cook Time: N/A

Serving: 1

Ingredients:

- 1 cup mixed berries (strawberries, blueberries, raspberries)
- 1/2 cup Greek yogurt
- 1 tablespoon honey
- 1/4 teaspoon cayenne pepper (adjust to taste)
- 1 cup almond milk
- 1 cup ice cubes

Instructions:

1. In a Nutribullet, combine Greek yogurt, honey, cayenne, and mixed berries.
2. You should include almond milk and ice cubes.
3. Lock the lid of the blender when the mixture is smooth and has a burst of berry taste, usually after 30-45 seconds of mixing on high.
4. Add some Berry Blast Metabolism Booster to a glass to speed up your metabolism.

TROPICAL PARADISE PROTEIN SHAKE

Preparation Time: 5 minutes

Cook Time: N/A

Serving: 1

Ingredients:

- 1/2 cup pineapple chunks
- 1/2 banana
- 1/2 cup coconut milk
- 1/2 cup Greek yogurt
- 1 scoop vanilla protein powder
- 1 tablespoon honey
- 1 cup ice cubes

Instructions:

1. The pineapple chunks, banana, coconut milk, Greek yogurt, vanilla protein powder, and honey should all be combined in a NutriBullet.
2. Add the ice cubes on top of the remaining ingredients.
3. Attach the cover to the blender, then mix the ingredients for 45 to 60 seconds on high or until they are smooth and flavorful of the tropics.
4. Pouring the Tropical Paradise Protein Shake into a glass will make you feel as though you're in a tropical paradise.

SPINACH AND PINEAPPLE SLIMDOWN

Preparation Time: 5 minutes

Cook Time: N/A

Serving: 1

Ingredients:

- 1 cup fresh spinach leaves
- 1/2 cup pineapple chunks
- 1/2 lime, juiced
- 1/4 avocado
- 1 tablespoon chia seeds
- 1 cup coconut water
- 1 cup ice cubes

Instructions:

1. In the NutriBullet blender, combine the chia seeds, avocado, pineapple chunks, lime juice, and fresh spinach leaves.
2. Coconut water and ice cubes should be included.
3. Blend the mixture on high for 45 to 60 seconds or until it is smooth and green while securing the cover of the blender.
4. To reduce weight in a healthy way, pour yourself a glass of Spinach and Pineapple Slimdown!

BLUEBERRY ALMOND BLISS

Preparation Time: 5 minutes

Cook Time: N/A

Serving: 1

Ingredients:

- 1/2 cup blueberries
- 1/4 cup almonds
- 1/2 cup Greek yogurt
- 1 tablespoon honey
- 1/2 teaspoon vanilla extract
- 1 cup almond milk
- 1 cup ice cubes

Instructions:

1. In a NutriBullet, you'll find blueberries, almonds, Greek yogurt, honey, and vanilla essence.
2. Add ice cubes and almond milk.
3. Put the blender on high for 30 to 45 seconds or until the mixture is entirely smooth and has the flavor of fresh blueberries.
4. Enjoy the flavor by pouring the Blueberry Almond Bliss into a glass.

CHOCOLATE PEANUT BUTTER POWERHOUSE

Preparation Time: 5 minutes

Cook Time: N/A

Serving: 1

Ingredients:

- 1 banana, peeled
- 2 tablespoons natural peanut butter
- 1 tablespoon cocoa powder
- 1 tablespoon honey
- 1 cup unsweetened almond milk
- 1 cup ice cubes

Instructions:

1. Bananas, natural peanut butter, chocolate powder, honey, and almond milk should all be blended in a NutriBullet.
2. Add the ice cubes on top of the remaining ingredients.
3. With the cover securely on, combine the ingredients for 30 to 45 seconds or until the sauce is deliciously smooth and chocolaty.
4. Take a sip of the delectable yet healthy Chocolate Peanut Butter Powerhouse to increase your energy.

KALE AND MANGO MAGIC

Preparation Time: 5 minutes

Cook Time: N/A

Serving: 1

Ingredients:

- 1 cup kale, stems removed
- 1/2 cup mango chunks
- 1/2 banana
- 1/2 lime, juiced
- 1 tablespoon honey
- 1 cup coconut water
- 1 cup ice cubes

Instructions:

1. Combine the kale, mango chunks, banana, lime juice, and honey in the Nutribullet mixer.
2. Coconut water and ice cubes should be included.
3. When the mixture is smooth and packed with the amazing flavor of kale and mango, lock the lid of the blender and blend it on high for 45 to 60 seconds.
4. Enjoy the enjoyment by adding some Kale and Mango Magic to a tumbler.

CUCUMBER MINT COOLER

Preparation Time: 5 minutes

Cook Time: N/A

Serving: 1

Ingredients:

- 1 cucumber, peeled and chopped
- 1/2 cup fresh mint leaves
- 1/2 lemon, juiced
- 1 tablespoon honey
- 1 cup water
- 1 cup ice cubes

Instructions:

1. Blend the cucumber, fresh mint leaves, lemon juice, and honey in the NutriBullet.
2. Add water and ice cubes.
3. Lock the blender cover and continue mixing till the liquid is silky and delightfully cooling, usually after around 30-45 seconds on high.
4. Pouring the Cucumber Mint Cooler into a glass is required. Enjoy this refreshing beverage to unwind.

PEANUT BUTTER BANANA SLIMMER

Preparation Time: 5 minutes

Cook Time: N/A

Serving: 1

Ingredients:

- 1 banana, peeled
- 1 tablespoon natural peanut butter
- 1/2 cup low-fat Greek yogurt
- 1/2 cup unsweetened almond milk
- 1 teaspoon honey (optional)
- 1/2 teaspoon ground cinnamon
- 1 cup ice cubes

Instructions:

1. Bananas, natural peanut butter, Greek yogurt, unsweetened almond milk, honey (if used), ground cinnamon, and ice cubes should all be combined in a Nutribullet blender.
2. When the mixture is smooth and chocolatey, blend it on high for 30 to 45 seconds with the lid firmly on the blender.
3. Pour the Peanut Butter Banana Slimmer into a glass to enjoy this delectable and successful slimming smoothie.

PAPAYA PASSION PROTEIN SHAKE

Preparation Time: 5 minutes

Cook Time: N/A

Serving: 1

Ingredients:

- 1 cup ripe papaya, peeled and cubed
- 1/2 cup plain
- 1/2 cup unsweetened coconut milk
- 1/4 cup fresh orange juice
- 1 tablespoon honey (optional)
- 1/2 teaspoon vanilla extract
- 1 cup ice cubes

Instructions:

1. Put the ripe papaya, protein powder, unsweetened coconut milk, fresh orange juice, honey (if used), vanilla extract, and ice cubes in your Nutribullet mixer and blend until smooth.
2. Put the blender's top on tightly and process the ingredients for 45 to 60 seconds on high or until the papaya is completely smooth.
3. Pour some of the Papaya Passion Protein Shake into a glass, and indulge in this delicious, protein-packed smoothie.

ALMOND JOY SMOOTHIE

Preparation Time: 5 minutes

Cook Time: N/A

Serving: 1

Ingredients:

- 1 ripe banana
- 1/4 cup shredded coconut
- 2 tablespoons cocoa powder
- 1 tablespoon almond butter
- 1 cup almond milk
- 1 tablespoon honey (optional)
- 1 cup ice cubes

Instructions:

1. Bananas, coconut flakes, cocoa powder, almond butter, almond milk, and honey (if used) should all be blended in a NutriBullet.
2. Add the ice cubes on top of the remaining ingredients.
3. With the top securely attached, blend the ingredients on high for 30 to 45 seconds or until it is smooth and creamy.
4. Pour the Almond Joy Smoothie into a glass, sprinkle with extra shredded coconut, and enjoy!

CITRUS SUNRISE ENERGIZER

Preparation Time: 5 minutes

Cook Time: 0 minutes

Serving: 1

Ingredients:

- 1 orange, peeled and segmented
- 1/2 grapefruit, peeled and segmented
- 1/2 lemon, peeled and juiced
- 1/2 lime, peeled and juiced
- 1 tablespoon honey or maple syrup (optional)
- 1 cup ice cubes

Instructions:

1. Begin by preparing the citrus fruits. Peel and segment the orange, peel and segment the grapefruit, and juice the lemon and lime.
2. Place all the prepared citrus fruits, lemon juice, lime juice, and honey (if using) into the Nutribullet blender.
3. Add the ice cubes on top of the other ingredients.
4. Secure the blender lid and blend on high until the mixture is smooth and the vibrant colors of the citrus fruits create a sunrise-like appearance. This should take about 45-60 seconds.
5. Taste the blend and adjust the sweetness with more honey or maple syrup if desired.
6. Pour the Citrus Sunrise Energizer into a glass, garnish with a citrus slice if you like, and sip on this invigorating and refreshing drink to kickstart your day with a burst of energy!

KIWI BERRY FAT BURNER

Preparation Time: 5 minutes

Cook Time: 0 minutes

Serving: 1

Ingredients:

- 2 kiwis, peeled and sliced
- 1/2 cup mixed berries
- 1/2 cup spinach leaves
- 1/2 cup Greek yogurt
- 1 tablespoon honey (optional)
- 1/4 cup water
- 1 cup ice cubes

Instructions:

1. The preparation processes include washing the berries, peeling and slicing the kiwis, and cleaning the spinach leaves.
2. In the Nutribullet mixer, combine the spinach leaves, Greek yogurt, kiwis, mixed berries, honey (if using), water, and ice cubes.
3. When the mixture is smooth and the vivid red and green colors are well-blended, secure the lid of the blender and turn it on high for 45 to 60 seconds.
4. The Kiwi Berry Fat Burner should be poured into a glass, and you can then enjoy this nutritious, antioxidant-rich smoothie, which can help boost metabolism.

VANILLA ALMOND DREAM

Preparation Time: 5 minutes

Cook Time: N/A

Serving: 1

Ingredients:

- 1 banana
- 1/2 teaspoon vanilla extract
- 1 tablespoon almond butter
- 1 cup almond milk
- 1 tablespoon honey (optional)
- 1 cup ice cubes

Instructions:

1. In the Nutribullet blender, combine the banana, ice cubes, almond milk, almond butter, vanilla extract, and honey (if using).
2. Secure the cover on the blender and process the mixture for 30 to 45 seconds on high or until it is smooth and dreamy.
3. Enjoy the creamy richness of the Vanilla Almond Dream after pouring it into a glass.

MANGO COCONUT BLISS

Preparation Time: 5 minutes

Cook Time: 0 minutes

Serving: 2

Ingredients:

- 1 cup frozen mango chunks
- 1/2 cup canned coconut milk
- 1/2 cup Greek yogurt
- 2 tablespoons honey
- 1/2 teaspoon vanilla extract
- 1/2 cup ice cubes (optional for a thicker consistency)

Instructions:

1. After gathering all of your components, clean your Nutribullet blender to ensure it is ready for use.
2. The frozen mango chunks should be added to the blender cup. If you want a thicker smoothie, add the ice cubes now.
3. Place the Greek yogurt, honey, vanilla bean paste, and canned coconut milk on top of the mango.
4. Carefully secure the blender's lid to avoid spills.
5. After around 30 to 45 seconds of high-speed mixing, the mixture ought to be creamy and smooth. If you've added ice cubes, give the mixture a little more time to combine to make sure the ice is well incorporated.
6. Once the Mango Coconut Bliss has been properly blended, remove the blender cup and carefully pour the smoothie into two serving glasses.
7. You may optionally add shredded coconut or a slice of mango to the top for a more tropical touch.
8. Right immediately, savor your hydrating and nutritious Mango Coconut Bliss smoothie.

CINNAMON ROLL SMOOTHIE

Preparation Time: 5 minutes

Cook Time: N/A

Serving: 1

Ingredients:

- 1/2 cup rolled oats
- 1 banana
- 1/2 teaspoon ground cinnamon
- 1 tablespoon honey
- 1 cup almond milk
- 1 cup ice cubes

Instructions:

1. In the Nutribullet blender, combine the almond milk, ice cubes, honey, rolled oats, banana, cinnamon powder, and crushed cloves.
2. Secure the blender's top and blend the mixture on high for 45 to 60 seconds or until it is smooth and tastes like a cinnamon bun.
3. Pour the cinnamon roll smoothie into a glass and enjoy the warming flavors!

BLUEBERRY AVOCADO ELIXIR

Preparation Time: 5 minutes

Cook Time: N/A

Serving: 1

Ingredients:

- 1/2 cup blueberries
- 1/2 ripe avocado
- 1/2 cup spinach leaves

- 1 tablespoon honey (optional)
- 1 cup almond milk
- 1 cup ice cubes

Instructions:

1. In the Nutribullet, combine the blueberries, ripe avocado, spinach, almond milk, ice cubes, and honey (if using).
2. With the lid firmly on the blender, blend the mixture for 30 to 45 seconds on high or until it is smooth and loaded with antioxidants.
3. The Blueberry Avocado Elixir's nutritious qualities may be enjoyed in a glass.

POMEGRANATE POWER PUNCH

Preparation Time: 5 minutes

Cook Time: 0 minutes

Serving: 1

Ingredients:

- 1/2 cup pomegranate seeds
- 1/2 cup Greek yogurt
- 1/2 cup unsweetened pomegranate juice
- 1/2 banana, peeled
- 1/4 cup rolled oats
- 1 tablespoon honey
- 1/2 teaspoon vanilla extract
- 1 cup ice cubes

Instructions:

1. Pomegranate seeds, Greek yogurt, unsweetened pomegranate juice, banana, rolled oats, honey, and vanilla extract should all be blended in a NutriBullet.
2. Add the ice cubes on top of the remaining ingredients.
3. Firmly fasten the blender's cover.
4. The mixture should be smooth and creamy after 45 to 60 seconds of high-speed mixing.
5. Pour the pomegranate power punch into a glass and savor its energizing, antioxidant-rich flavors.

CHOCOLATE CHERRY CHIA SHAKE

Preparation Time: 5 minutes

Cook Time: N/A

Serving: 1

Ingredients:

- 1/2 cup frozen cherries
- 1 tablespoon unsweetened cocoa powder
- 1 tablespoon chia seeds

- 1 tablespoon honey (optional)
- 1 cup almond milk
- 1 cup ice cubes

Instructions:

1. Blend the frozen cherries, cocoa powder, chia seeds, honey (if using), almond milk, and ice cubes in the Nutribullet.
2. The mixture should be smooth, rich, and chocolaty after 30 to 45 seconds of high-speed blending. Close the blender's lid.
3. Enjoy this delicious delight by filling a glass with the Chocolate Cherry Chia Shake!

MATCHA GREEN TEA REVITALIZER

Preparation Time: 5 minutes

Cook Time: N/A

Serving: 1

Ingredients:

- 1 teaspoon matcha green tea powder
- 1 banana
- 1/2 cup spinach leaves
- 1/2 cup Greek yogurt
- 1 tablespoon honey (optional)
- 1 cup almond milk
- 1 cup ice cubes

Instructions:

1. Matcha green tea powder, banana, spinach leaves, Greek yogurt, honey (if used), almond milk, and ice cubes should all be blended in a NutriBullet.
2. Blend the mixture on high for 30 to 45 seconds, or until it turns a vivid, energizing green, after securing the blender's cover.
3. After pouring the Matcha Green Tea Revitalizer into a glass, feel the positive health boost!

MIXED BERRY ANTIOXIDANT BOOST

Preparation Time: 5 minutes

Cook Time: N/A

Serving: 2

Ingredients:

- 1 cup mixed berries (strawberries, blueberries, raspberries)
- 1/2 cup plain Greek yogurt
- 1/2 cup unsweetened almond milk
- 2 tablespoons honey
- 1/2 teaspoon chia seeds (optional)
- 1 cup ice cubes

Instructions:

1. The mixed berries, Greek yogurt, almond milk, honey, and chia seeds (if used) should all be added to the Nutribullet mixer.
2. Add the ice cubes on top of the remaining ingredients.
3. Put the blender's cover on tightly and process the mixture for 45 to 60 seconds on high or until it is smooth and the color of a bright cherry.
4. Pour the Mixed Berry Antioxidant Boost into two glasses for a reviving and antioxidant-rich smoothie.

PINEAPPLE COCONUT PROTEIN PARADISE

Preparation Time: 5 minutes

Cook Time: N/A

Serving: 1

Ingredients:

- 1/2 cup pineapple chunks (fresh or frozen)
- 1/2 ripe banana
- 1/2 cup coconut milk
- 1/4 cup vanilla protein powder
- 1 tablespoon shredded coconut (optional)
- 1/2 cup ice cubes

Instructions:

1. Place the NutriBullet blender on top of the banana, pineapple chunks, coconut milk, vanilla protein powder, and (if using) shredded coconut.
2. Add the ice cubes on top of the remaining ingredients.
3. Ensure that the blender lid is securely positioned and proceed to mix the components for a duration of 45-60 seconds or until a homogeneous and velvety texture is achieved.
4. Pour the Pineapple Coconut Protein Paradise into a glass, top with extra shredded coconut if you want, and savor!

STRAWBERRY BANANA SWIRL

Preparation Time: 5 minutes

Cook Time: N/A

Serving: 1

Ingredients:

- 1/2 cup strawberries, hulled
- 1 ripe banana
- 1/2 cup plain Greek yogurt
- 1 tablespoon honey
- 1/4 cup water
- 1/2 teaspoon vanilla extract
- 1 cup ice cubes

Instructions:

1. Strawberries, bananas, Greek yogurt, honey, water, and vanilla extract should all be combined in a NutriBullet.
2. Add the ice cubes on top of the remaining ingredients.
3. Secure the blender's lid, then mix for 45 to 60 seconds on high or until the liquid is smooth and the red and yellow have been tastefully incorporated.
4. Pour the Strawberry Banana Swirl into a glass and sip on this refreshing and delightful smoothie.

ALMOND CARAMEL CRUNCH

Preparation Time: 5 minutes

Cook Time: N/A

Serving: 1

Ingredients:

- 1 ripe banana
- 1/2 cup unsweetened almond milk
- 1 tablespoon almond butter
- 1 Medjool date, pitted

- 1/2 teaspoon vanilla extract
- 1 tablespoon caramel syrup (sugar-free if preferred)
- 1/4 cup rolled oats
- 1 cup ice cubes

Instructions:

1. The ripe banana, unsweetened almond milk, almond butter, pitted Medjool dates, vanilla extract, caramel syrup, rolled oats, and ice cubes should all be added to the Nutribullet blender.
2. Blend the mixture on high for 45 to 60 seconds or until it is creamy and smooth while securing the cover of the blender.
3. Pour Almond Caramel Crunch into a glass, top with more caramel syrup if desired, and savor!

CRANBERRY ORANGE DETOXIFIER

Preparation Time: 5 minutes

Cook Time: N/A

Serving: 1

Ingredients:

- 1/2 cup fresh cranberries
- 1 orange, peeled and segmented
- 1/2 cup Greek yogurt
- 1 tablespoon honey
- 1/2 teaspoon grated ginger
- 1/2 cup water
- 1 cup ice cubes

Instructions:

1. Fresh cranberries, an orange that has been peeled and cut into segments, Greek yogurt, honey, ginger that has been diced, water, and ice cubes should all be added to the Nutribullet mixer.
2. Put the lid on the blender and process for 45 to 60 seconds on high, or until the mixture is smooth and the cranberry and brilliant orange tones are merged.
3. After adding the Cranberry Orange Detoxifier to a glass, savor this delicious and detoxifying smoothie.

ACAI BERRY BEAUTY BOOSTER

Preparation Time: 5 minutes

Cook Time: N/A

Serving: 1

Ingredients:

- 1 packet of frozen acai berry puree (unsweetened)
- 1/2 cup mixed berries (e.g., blueberries, strawberries, raspberries)
- 1/2 cup unsweetened almond milk
- 1 tablespoon honey or agave nectar
- 1/4 cup Greek yogurt
- 1/2 teaspoon chia seeds
- 1 cup ice cubes

Instructions:

1. The frozen acai berry puree should be divided into smaller pieces before being blended in a NutriBullet with frozen mixed berries, unsweetened almond milk, honey or agave nectar, Greek yogurt, chia seeds, and ice cubes.
2. Secure the blender's cover before blending the ingredients on high for 45–60 seconds or until they are thick and smooth like a smoothie.
3. Pour the Acai Berry Beauty Booster into a glass, top with additional chia seeds if preferred, and enjoy this smoothie packed with antioxidants that will make you look better!

APPLE CINNAMON WEIGHT MANAGER

Preparation Time: 5 minutes

Cook Time: N/A

Serving: 1

Ingredients:

- 1 medium apple, cored and chopped
- 1/2 teaspoon ground cinnamon
- 1/4 cup rolled oats
- 1 cup unsweetened almond milk
- 1 tablespoon honey or maple syrup (optional)
- 1/2 teaspoon vanilla extract
- 1 cup ice cubes

Instructions:

1. Diced apple, ground cinnamon, rolled oats, almond milk, honey (if used), vanilla extract, and ice cubes should all be combined in a Nutribullet blender.
2. Blend the mixture on high for 45–60 seconds, or until it is smooth and the oats are well incorporated while locking the cover of the blender.
3. To aid in weight management, the Apple Cinnamon Weight Manager should be poured into a glass, sprinkled with a little cinnamon, and consumed.

CHOCOLATE MINT SLIM SHAKE

Preparation Time: 5 minutes

Cook Time: N/A

Serving: 1

Ingredients:

- 1 cup unsweetened almond milk
- 1 scoop of chocolate protein powder
- 1 tablespoon cocoa powder
- 1/4 teaspoon peppermint extract
- 1/2 banana, peeled
- 1 tablespoon fresh mint leaves
- 1 cup ice cubes

Instructions:

1. Combine the almond milk, chocolate protein powder, cocoa powder, peppermint essence, banana, fresh mint leaves, and ice cubes in the Nutribullet mixer.
2. Set the blender's lid in place and blend on high for typically 30 to 45 seconds, or until the mixture is smooth and strongly flavorful of chocolate and mint.
3. Pour the Chocolate Mint Slim beverage into a glass, top with a mint leaf, and savor this satisfying and delicious beverage to support your weight reduction efforts!

THE END